LIFE ON THE AIRLINERS

For Lynne

With fond memories of

a shared experience on

Christmas Day 1990!!!

Bob Price

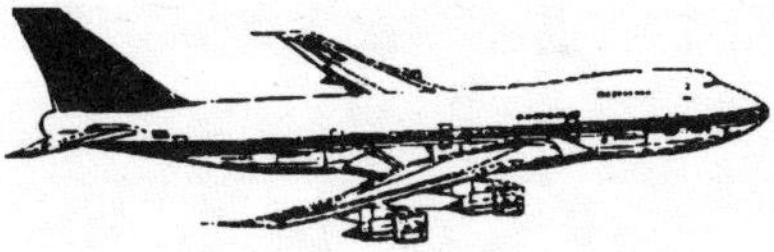

LIFE ON THE AIRLINERS

By
Bob Price

BROOKS

Brooks Books
England

Published in Great Britain by Brooks Books, 23 Sylvan Avenue,
Bitterne, Southampton, Hampshire, SO2 5JW, England.

British Library Cataloguing in Publication Data
Price, Robert, *1945.*
Life on the Airliners
1. Air passenger transport services, history.
I. Title
387 .7420904
ISBN 1 872706 06 1

Printed in the Channel Islands by the Guernsey Press.
Trade distribution through Ruskin Book Services, Kidderminster

Whilst we have striven for accuracy throughout this project, it has not always been possible to verify exact quotes used at the time of various incidents. For this we can only apologise and stress that every effort has been made in pursuit of this end. The quotes used in those cases are the author's own interpretation of the dialogue that may have taken place under the given circumstances. Additionally, we have made every effort to contact copyright owners where applicable. However, any omissions will be gladly rectified in future editions.

Programme of Events

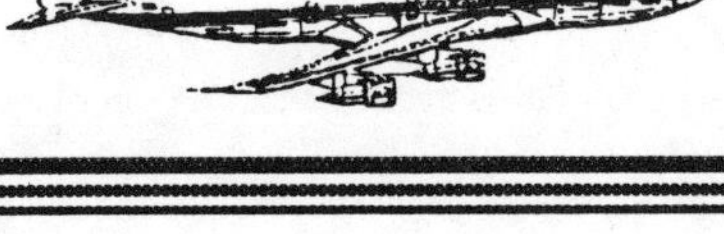

This book is for
my wife, Sue,
for all the
happy years.

FOREWORD

'Life on the Airliners' is a flying book with a difference. Far removed from the usual specialist type of aviation publication, it offers a unique insight into the fascinating world of air travel and lays waste to the theory that all of us involved in it are perfection personified!

From the early days of the wooden bi-plane airliners, to the supersonic era of Concorde, Bob has produced a highly readable account of the men and women whose adventures, both dramatic and funny, will delight fliers and earthbound types alike for their bold content.

High drama combines with wicked humour to present a hugely enjoyable mixture of danger and laughter that will find favour in all quarters. Pilots, stewardesses, customs officers, passengers – all have come forward to relate their stories in vivid detail, allowing the reader to embark on a journey of pure escapism from which they will not wish to return until the last page has been turned.

'Life on the Airliners' is not a history book, yet the first chapter takes an entertaining and informative look at the various airlines as they battled through their formative years. It really is a must for anyone who enjoys a good, old fashioned yarn.

Eric Moody

Captain Eric H. J. Moody
British Airways

ACKNOWLEDGEMENTS

Research, for a book of this nature, can often prove a lengthy and arduous task if the necessary information is not readily forthcoming. My everlasting gratitude is assured to every individual and company, far too numerous to mention, who gave their time and full support to make my job not only easy, but a real pleasure.

Special thanks to Peter Boyd-Smith of *Cobwebs* memorabilia store in Southampton, for supplying some of the cover materials, Messrs. Eric Moody, Tim Lancaster, 'Tommy' Thompson, Tom Wright and Clarrie Moore – intrepid aviators all, who provided much needed assistance when called upon. To John Bowley for the excellent cartoons, to Nan Witcomb and Judy Davis, the girls from 'down under' and fellow countryman, John White of Qantas Airways, who never failed to meet my incessant demands with courtesy and promptness. Thanks also to Michelle Gagne of Air Canada for her kindness and help, to British Airways for the assistance provided, and finally to Gilbert Denton and the Commissioners of Her Majesty's Customs and Excise for their hospitality and invaluable help on the last chapter.

The following authors and publishers, likewise, have given their permission for the use of certain material in their own books:

Airlife Publishing Ltd – *'Crisis on the Flightdeck'*
© Stanley Stewart 1989.
Sidgwick and Jackson Ltd – *'Animals by Air'*
© Neville Whittaker 1983.
Corgi Books by Transworld Publishers Ltd –
'The Ghost of Flight 401' © John Fuller 1976.
Hamlyn Publishing – *'Pan Am, an Airline and its Aircraft'*
Text and maps © R.E.G Davies 1987
'Up Here and Down There"© Nan Whitcomb. Obtainable from
PO Box 230, Brighton, South Australia, 5048.

NOTE: For various reasons, I have changed the names of certain people featured in this book. In those cases where a name has been changed, an asterisk (*) will appear alongside it in the text.

Chapter 1

Out of the Ashes

At full throttle the *Benoist 14* flying boat thundered across the once calm waters of Florida's Tampa Bay, a foaming, hissing bow wave marking its shuddering progress. For pilot, Tony Jannus and his solitary passenger, the deafening roar of the huge *'pusher'* engine looming behind their tiny cockpit lent a note of urgency to the occasion as the aircraft's massive twin wings sought desperately for the sanctuary of flight. The hot, oily smell of an over-straining engine engulfed the two men as, with a sudden leap, the flying boat rose jubilantly into the air, water cascading from its sharply angled fuselage.

The year was 1914 – January the 1st. Flying under the banner of the St. Petersburg – Tampa Airboat Line, Tony Jannus led his company into the history books as the first airline ever to provide a scheduled air passenger service.

Although the St. Petersburg – Tampa Airboat Line, founded by an imaginative and adventurous man by the name of Percy Fansler, had a relatively short operational life of only three months, it demonstrated to the world that the safe carriage of passengers by air, for profit, was a feasible proposition. The company flew over a thousand passengers (one at a time) across the eighteen mile stretch of water at a cost of five dollars a head. Expensive? Certainly, by 1914 standards, but considered money well spent by the airline's customers, weary of the tortuous thirty six mile surface trip around the bay.

For Tony Jannus, sadly killed in the First World War that followed closely on the heels of his peaceful inaugural flight across Tampa Bay, there could be no inkling of the scope and size of the giant global airliners that were to follow in his slipstream, yet the seal had been set on that bright January morning in 1914 for one of the most fascinating ventures in aviation history – the transportation of passengers, by air, to destinations once deemed so remote as to be practically inaccessible.

The Great War of 1914-18 effectively halted the advancement of civil flying and the development of the aeroplane as a weapon of war took priority over its commercial potential. At the end of the conflict, the fields of France were littered with the remains of beautiful and legendary machines, sent tumbling from the skies in an orgy of self-destruction. Tommy Sopwith's *Camels, Snipes* and *Pups;* Anthony Fokker's *triplanes* and *DV11s;* the French *Nieuports* and *Spads* – all flown by aviators who shared a common bond – the fellowship of the air.

The end of the war found many of these young men eager to carry on flying, and from out of the ashes of that terrible conflict sprang the seeds of today's mighty airlines. From the poppy fields of Flanders, they drifted home to the green pastures of England; the plains and great cities of America; the defeated towns of Germany; the outback of Australia – all looking to friendlier skies and the chance to fly in peace.

Early attempts at passenger transportation, in hastily modified warplanes, posed no threat whatsoever to the livelihoods of those whose business revolved around rail, road or sea travel. To be borne aloft in machines of dubious stability with the added disadvantage of being deafened and sprayed with oil in the process took more than a little courage. To be asked to pay for the privilege, not to mention the freezing discomfort, was deemed by most to be foolhardy in the extreme.

To ensure that passengers arrived at their destinations in a reasonable state of consciousness, it was necessary for the early airlines to provide them with a wardrobe of leather flying coats, gloves, helmets, goggles and, in exceptionally chilly weather, a hot water bottle. Hip flasks, with built in warmth and courage, became the favourite travelling companion of many a shivering passenger.

It quickly became apparent that to attract customers away from the more conventional means of travel, airlines had to be able to offer a very large degree of safety and comfort if they were to be considered serious rivals to their land and sea based competitors. Several aircraft began to come off the drawing board, designed specifically with the comfort and well-being of the passenger in mind. In Germany, Deutsche Luft-Reederei (later, Lufthansa) who had achieved the distinction of becoming the first operational airline to provide a sustained passenger service (Berlin to Weimar) took delivery of several *AEJ J11* Biplanes to replace their open-cockpit *LVGs* and proudly offered its passengers an enclosed five-seater saloon type compartment for their comfort.

Justifiably proud of their revolutionary new fleet, Deutsche Luft-Reederei decided to adorn all of their aircraft with a distinguishing emblem. The design they chose, a crane in flight, remains to this day as the fleet emblem of Lufthansa.

In Britain the Westland *Limousine*, winner of the Air Ministry Commercial Aeroplane Competition, sought to bring to the airways a touch of the luxury attributed to its motorised namesake. Fitted with four deeply comfortable and well upholstered armchairs, it became one of the earliest 'executive' airliners when Westland's managing director dictated letters to his personal secretary whilst in flight.

Gradually, like a slowly spinning propeller gathering momentum, the embryos of today's majestic airlines began to emerge from the awakening new industry. AT&T (Aircraft Transport and Travel), Handley Page Transport and Instone Airlines dominated the British scene, with AT&T taking the honours for operating the first regular scheduled international daily air service between Hounslow and Le Brouget in Paris. This unique milestone took place on 25th August, 1919 when a *De Havilland 16* under the command of Major Cyril Patterson took off from Hounslow with four fare-paying passengers who had parted with the not inconsiderable sum of £21 for the one way flight. The rail/boat fare to Paris at this time stood at £3 8s 5p!

Handley Page, beaten to the cross-Channel punch by eight days, sought to quickly redress the balance by immediately undercutting AT&T's fare to £15 15s single and £31 10s return – a substantial reduction that delighted their many passengers. They also introduced in-flight meals at a cost of three shillings a head. These came in the form of lunchboxes and contained several tasty sandwiches, a bar of chocolate and assorted fruit – a feast that the majority found hard to stomach in the bouncing, lurching machines that carried them!

The wind of change, however, began to blow cold across the necks of the British companies with the arrival of the heavily subsidised foreign airlines on the cross-channel scene. The French, for instance, were able to offer a London – Paris crossing for just six guineas – a sum that the British, with no Government backing, found impossible to match. AT&T quickly went out of business and Handley Page were forced to abandon their regular cross-channel services.

By February, 1921 all the UK airlines had ceased operations, with AT&T eventually going bankrupt. The foreign companies enjoyed the sole use of all the British aerodromes, a state of affairs that eventually stirred the British Government into belated action. They injected a massive subsidy into civil aviation allowing Handley Page and Instone to resume cross-channel operations at competitive rates.

> *Daimler Airways, who filled the gap left by AT&T, pioneered another 'first' in passenger aviation when they appointed fourteen year–old boys to act as flight attendants. Specially trained at London's exclusive Savoy Hotel and resplendent in full page-boy uniforms, they were nonetheless restricted in the service they could offer –notably due to the fact that they were forced to remain seated throughout the duration of the flight!*

On the other side of the world, meanwhile, strange events were unfolding that would eventually bring about the formation of one of the world's greatest airlines.

Two young war veterans, Lts P.J. (Paul) McGuinness and W. (Wilmott) Hudson-Fysh, late of the Australian Flying Corps, found themselves bouncing around the Queensland outback in an ancient *Model T* Ford, checking part of the proposed route for an England–Australia air race. Unable to afford the entrance fee themselves, the luckless duo cursed every bone-jarring mile of their trip and had no difficulty convincing each other that the only civilised way to cross such a barren and hostile landscape was by aircraft. They were to find a receptive ear for their ideas in the unlikely but commanding form of Fergus McMaster, manager of the Devoncourt sheep and cattle station.

Fergus had been elected as chairman of the Cloncurry *'Anti-cattle duffing'* association, formed to thwart the attentions of rustlers who were plaguing the area with an outbreak of *'Poddy Dodging'*. This practice of stealing young calves that had yet to be branded had reached epidemic proportions and it was whilst engaged on these duties that destiny pushed him into a meeting that was to alter the course of history.

A broken axle in the middle of the Cloncurry River sent the wet and raging manager stomping off in search of help – conveniently waiting in the form of a hard-up, but enterprising, Paul McGuiness. The intrepid flyer quickly obtained spares and mounted a successful rescue operation to recover the submerged car. The two men struck up a friendship that came to fruition in 1920 when McGuiness, accompanied by Hudson-Fysh, approached Fergus with the idea of setting up an aviation company to service north-east Australia.

With the aid of fellow business partners, Fergus set up the Queensland and Northern Territory Aerial Services Ltd on November 16th 1920. Almost immediately it acquired a shortened name based on the company initials – a name that has since proudly flown the Australian flag throughout the world – QANTAS.

Elsewhere, problems beset even the mightiest of nations. In the United States of America, Aeromarine, a company formed shortly after the First World War, began flying converted navy *F-5L* flying boats capable of carrying up to fourteen fare-paying passengers. In 1920, the airline took over Florida West Indies Airways and began operations as Aeromarine West Indies Airways.

Despite an impressive and accident-free safety record, the airline folded in 1923 leaving America, ironically, trailing behind the rest of the world in the field of passenger aviation – a situation they were to rectify with a vengeance in later years.

KLM (Royal Dutch Airlines). Founded in 1919 this famous airline is the oldest company in the world still flying under its original name. Unique though this distinction is, it doesn't prevent some of its regular British passengers from affectionately referring to their journey as, "Flying with the 'Old Dutch' "

Imperial Airways

On the 1st April, 1924, Great Britain entered an era of majestic and adventurous pioneering when British Marine Air Navigation Company, Daimler Airways, Handley Page Transport and Instone Airlines merged to form Imperial Airways. Glorious chapters in aviation history were to be written by Imperial's men and machines in the coming years, but the early days gave little indication of the glory that was to follow. It began with a pilots strike over pay and conditions – a dispute that delighted the foreign companies who suddenly found themselves fully booked on every flight.

Even with the dispute settled, problems beset the airline from other angles. Complaints began to drop through the letterbox from angry residents living in the vicinity of airfield runways. Residents who were considerably alarmed at the increase in air traffic and the frighteningly low height at which some of the aircraft flew as they struggled for altitude.

Gradually the problems were ironed out and Imperial began to look beyond their European routes in a determined effort to extend the long arm of British aviation. A survey flight to India resulted in the eventual opening of a UK – India route in 1929 at a cost of £130 per passenger. The journey took seven days, with passengers transferring to a train for the Basle to Genoa leg (Italy would not permit foreign aircraft to enter their airspace from France, and the Alps were considered too dangerous to fly over)

Imperial Airways desert fuel dumps were of great interest to Arab tribesmen during this period, and extreme precautions were taken to protect them from marauding bands. The tribesmen, having witnessed the re-fuelling and departure of Imperial's aircraft, became convinced that their camels would sprout wings and bear them aloft if they drank of the 'magic water'.

'Five goatskins of unleaded please!'

With the opening of its long-range routes, Imperial Airways decided that passenger comfort was now an absolute priority and ordered a new type of aircraft that would go into history as the first four-engined airliner to go into regular service. This aircraft was to be compared, in terms of luxury, to the great ocean-going Cunarders gracing the transport scene at the time.

The *Handley Page 42 (HP42)* was a magnificent machine in every respect apart from one. It was considered by many to be too slow. With its huge wings and massive un-cowled engines, jibes were often directed at its 'built-in headwinds', and there could be no denying the claim. It was not unusual for the *HP42* to be overtaken by passenger trains as it flew unhurriedly on to its destination.

The critics however, were howled down as the *HP42* more than compensated for its lack of speed in many other ways. Designed to provide a high standard of comfort, the aircraft's 'two-tier' engine settings reduced noise and vibration levels considerably whilst the cabin furnishings would not have been out of place in a stately mansion.

The first of these incredible aeroplanes (eight only were built at a cost of £20,000 each) lumbered out of its hangar in 1930. Proudly bearing the name, *Hannibal* it was to be joined later by, *Hadrian, Horatius, Hengist, Helena, Heracles, Hanno* and *Horsea*. Noble names that lent an air of heroic majesty to the airliners that would later be able to boast that, in almost ten years service, not a single passenger would be lost or injured whilst on a *HP42*.

Imagine, for a moment, that you are about to board an *HP42* for the flight of a lifetime. As you cross the airfield apron, the huge airliner dominates the scene with its four massive Bristol *Jupiter* engines ready to burst into life at a moment's notice. Almost ninety feet from nose to tail with an even bigger wingspan of one hundred and thirty feet, it looks indestructible.

A steward, immaculate in whites, welcomes you aboard with a reassuring word and guides you to your allocated seat. Deep piled carpets covering the entire floor area and the cabin's tastefully panelled interior blend to create a warm, cosy atmosphere in which to undertake your journey in style.

Seating arrangements are suitably in line with the surroundings with large armchairs provided to ensure maximum comfort. Fragrant, fresh-cut flowers in silver vases adorn the tables separating you from your fellow passengers—tables large enough to accommodate the hot, tasty four-course meals that will be provided during the flight. The finest linen, china, silver cutlery and crystal wine glasses set the seal on one of the most elegant services of its kind. Quality wines of excellent vintage to accompany the sumptuous meal will mellow even the most nervous of travellers. Finally, as the great machine lifts sedately into the air and your captain eases back on the control column to gain cruising height, draw back the pure silk curtains that cover the wide cabin windows and enjoy the unequalled beauty of a green, patchwork quilted English countryside as it slides peacefully by.

A rigorous no-smoking rule was enforced on the HP42s in an endeavour to remove the risk of accidental fire. Imperial Airways set a fine of two hundred pounds and six months imprisonment for offenders. Only one passenger was ever taken to court for refusing to extinguish the cigarettes he chain-smoked throughout his flight to Paris. He received only a ten pound fine.

The great era of Imperial's empire flying boats began in 1934 when they took one of the biggest gambles in aviation history by ordering twenty-eight *Short 'C' class* aircraft to operate along their eastern routes.

Huge, wonderfully adaptable machines, the *'C' class* boats provided an exceptionally high standard of spacious comfort. With two decks, a smoke-room and promenade saloon, passengers were able to stretch their legs and enjoy the pleasures normally reserved for ocean-going liners.

Operations began in 1937, with services from Southampton to Alexandria, closely followed by the African run, flown solely by flying boats. Even America benefitted from Imperial's services, when one of their fleet, *Cavalier* was shipped to Bermuda to begin a regular New York shuttle.

During its sixteen year reign, Imperial Airways opened up a network of routes that included the Middle East, South Africa, India and Australia. The latter route, operated in conjunction with Qantas Empire Airways, covered 13,000 miles and took a stamina-sapping twelve days to complete—it was not a journey for the faint-hearted.

During the overnight stop on the desert leg of the flight, passengers would be accommodated in a magnificent Foreign Legion style fort at Rutbah Wells, midway between Amman and Baghdad. This was not a gimmick to add a touch of romance to the journey, but a very real necessity to protect Imperial's passengers from the threat of attack by fierce desert gangs . Guarded by armed soldiers, the travellers could relax and enjoy the luxury of a hot bath or shower to ease their aching limbs.

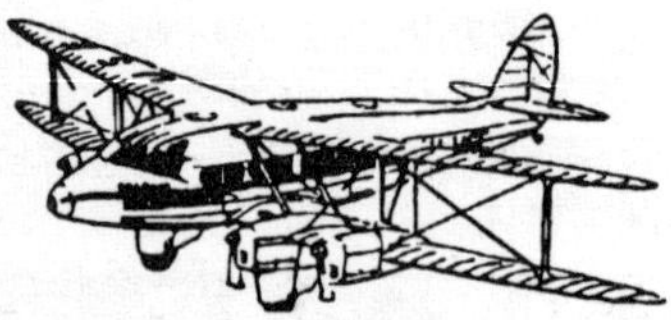
DH 86

The final stage of the journey, in a De Havilland *A86* biplane, took them across the Timor Sea to Australia. It was widely held that no passenger, however tired, ever slept whilst being borne across this shark-infested stretch of water!

The illustrious reign of Imperial Airways drew to a close just before the outbreak of World War Two when it was absorbed into BOAC. The adventure was over, but the traditions of care and service forged by the men and machines of Imperial's trail-blazing fleet were to set a high standard of impeccable quality that many airlines would find extremely hard to emulate.

The American Challenge

Arriving late on the international passenger-carrying scene, the Americans finally entered the fray in March 1927 with the formation of Pan American Airways.

It's hard to imagine that a giant corporation like Pan American nearly fell at the first hurdle during its formative early days, but that's exactly what happened. The story and the amazing stroke of good fortune that saved the day is now part of American aviation folklore.

During the tense and nerve-wracking period prior to Pan American's acceptance as a legitimate route-flying airline, a serious situation developed over a mail contract deadline. The contract, vital to the airline's credibility and potential, called for mail to be taken from Key West to Havana by the deadline date of 19th October, 1927. Unfortunately, Pan American's *Fokker F VII* landplane could not take off from the rubble-strewn, incomplete, airfield at Key West and frustration ran high among the ranks of the struggling airline.

Salvation, in the form of a *Fairchild FC-2* floatplane belonging to West Indian Aerial Express, splashed-down at Key West enroute for Havana. The aeroplane's pilot had interrupted his journey to check out weather reports indicating an impending hurricane.

Hearing of the floatplane's arrival a Pan American representative raced to the scene, his pockets bulging with company dollars. Minutes later, the wad of notes changed hands – West Indies Aerial Express *Fairchild* was now on charter to Pan American.

The hurricane failed to show, the mail was delivered with time to spare and an airline that was to become one of the finest in the world finally got off the ground.

Developments in the field of civil aviation began to surge forward in leaps and bounds with the arrival of the Americans, with Pan Am favouring flying boats for the majority of its services. The advantages of safety and convenience, they felt, outweighed the hazards of transferring passengers from shore to aeroplane in small boats. Many a shaken passenger, perilously tossed about in an open boat in choppy seas, found that any fear of flying they may have harboured beforehand had completely disappeared by the time they were safely on board.

The first of Pan Am's famous *Clipper* flying boats, a *Sikorsky S-40*, took to the air in 1931 carrying eight passengers in elegant style. It contributed a great deal towards the promotion of flying boats as the ideal mode of air transport and led America into one of its most exciting achievements – Atlantic supremacy.

The instrument of this achievement, the *Boeing 314* flying boat, outshone all its rivals in both size and power and was destined never to be challenged as the Neptune of the skies, when, in 1939, Pan American's *Yankee Clipper* flew the first scheduled transatlantic airline service.

Flying between Botwood, Newfoundland and Southampton, Yankee Clipper took eighteen hours and forty-two minutes to complete the journey at a cost of one hundred and forty pounds return.

The standard of comfort afforded *Yankee Clipper's* nineteen passengers has yet to be equalled and, unfortunately, it was to prove the final 'grand gesture' that signalled the end of flying-boat supremacy throughout the world. Aside from its separate cabins, a recreation lounge, dining saloon, ladies dressing room and comfortable sleeping berths were provided for the comfort and entertainment of the privileged few. However, By far the most outstanding piece of self-indulgence ever installed in a passenger aircraft had to be *Yankee Clipper's* luxurious, much sought after, bridal suite – a truly romantic touch that was well in keeping with the traditions of the flying-boat era. The cat, however, was already among the pigeons:

In 1938, one year prior to *Yankee Clipper's* historic flight, a *Focke-Wulf FW200 Condor* took- off from Berlin and flew non-stop to New York with twelve passengers on board – the first aircraft to successfully display the advantages of landplane operations. The obvious benefits of boarding passengers straight from the comfort of an airfield terminal building and with the coming war about to provide the paved runways needed for long-range aircraft, the days of the flying boat were numbered.

The first airline to offer its passengers the choice of first or second class travel was Imperial Airways. In 1927, first class passengers were transported between London and Paris on board Silver Wing Argosies at a cost of nine pounds. The journey, with steward service and all the trimmings, took two hours thirty minutes. The cost of thrift for second class passengers (seven pounds ten shillings) was a three hour trip in a lurching Handley Page bi-plane without the benefit of food or drink or the ministrations of a caring steward.

At this stage of the game, several airlines were up and running, spreading their wings over both domestic and global air corridors. Lufthansa bore its famous name aloft in 1926 whilst TWA (Trans World Airlines), United, Northwest, Continental, Eastern, American and Delta Airlines, contested the American scene with Pan American.

The Russian effort centred around the government owned Dobroflot, re-named Aeroflot in 1932. Air France rose from the merger of five transport operators in 1933, eventually becoming one of Europe's largest airlines.

Ansett Airlines, founded in 1936, graced the Australian scene alongside Qantas and, on the other side of the world, momentous events were unfolding that would see the emergence of yet another great airline – Air Canada.

Canada, with its vast open spaces and unforgiving climate, proved a difficult frontier to conquer for the country's only major passenger airline. Extreme temperatures and rugged terrain (The Rocky Mountains had hitherto been negotiated by aircraft flying through their forbidding peaks, as opposed to going over them) presented, problems that, at times, seemed insurmountable. The Canadians tough and outspoken spirit won the day and, in the course of their remarkable progress, they managed to notch up several important 'firsts' in passenger aviation.

During the latter part of the 1930's they became the first airline to equip their entire fleet of unpressurized aircraft with oxygen masks to allow them to overfly the Rocky Mountains. The system was not without its teething problems though.

The job of assisting passengers to fit and adjust their oxygen masks fell, not surprisingly, to the airline's stewardesses and it was here that the problem presented itself. Without the benefit of extension tubes, the girls were obliged to remove their own masks whilst carrying out these duties and, on more than one occasion, passengers were called upon to help revive an oxygen-starved stewardess who had collapsed in an undignified heap on the floor of the aircraft.

Another first for the Canadians was the introduction of de-icing equipment on the front windscreens of all their aircraft – an indication of the problems presented by the country's harsh climate.

The 1930s saw rapid advances in aircraft design and the lumbering bi-planes that had dominated the skies during the early days of civil aviation faded into history – to be replaced by machines that would write their own chapters in the exciting saga of air travel.

The *Boeing 247*, with its retractable undercarriage, cantilever low-wings and all-metal structure is generally regarded as the first true ancestor of the modern airliner and, with a cruising speed of 180mph, outstripped its rivals by a good 50mph.

Introducing, as it did, a new age in passenger aviation, the *247* was nonetheless overshadowed by the unveiling of a new type of aircraft in July 1933. The aircraft itself did not attract a great deal of comment at the time, in fact, only one was built, but from it there sprang two sister ships that were to wing their way into the hearts of both flyers and passengers throughout the world. The aircraft was a *Douglas DC-1.* Its successors were the *DC-2* and the wider bodied *DC-3* – the famous *Dakota.*

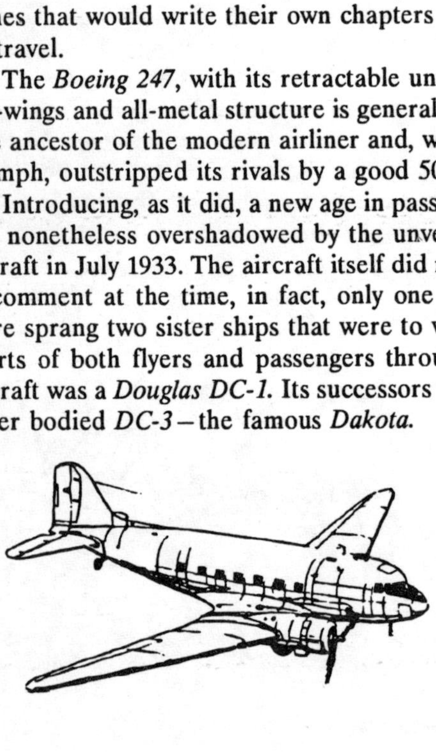

The impact the *DC-3* was to have on the world of commercial aviation quickly became apparent when it entered service in 1935. Airline representatives literally queued at the door to place their orders for the revolutionary new aircraft and, in 1936, recognition of its popularity came in the form of the Collier Trophy for the outstanding twin-engined commercial transport aeroplane of the year.

Thousands upon thousands of these remarkable aeroplanes were manufactured during the period up to and including the Second World War, with airlines throughout the world snapping up all surplus stocks at the end of hostilities.

To this day, well over fifty years on, the *DC-3* is still flying operationally in some corners of the globe – a fitting tribute to an aeroplane that introduced a significant degree of quiet comfort to passenger transportation and then went on to become the work-horse of the skies.

The 1930s drew to a close with a final flourish when the *Boeing 307 Stratoliner* soared high into the air as the first passenger aircraft equipped with a pressurized cabin. Passengers could now look forward to being flown safely over most rough weather conditions without the need for claustrophobic oxygen masks.

After the Conflict

Six years of war forced the manufacture of civilian airliners to a virtual standstill, with America alone producing large numbers of transport aircraft to meet the demands of the Allied Forces.

At the end of the conflict, as in the First World War, converted military bombers formed the backbone of many post-war airlines and provided the precious breathing space needed for the design and construction of new commercial airliners.

The Lockheed Constellation

Some of these new airliners had been in the design and development stage prior to the war's end and were to meet with widely differing fortunes. Lockheed's *Constellations*, for instance, were a revelation with their sleek 'Greyhound' lines and superior airspeed. It would be *'Connies'* of Pan American and

American Overseas Airlines that were to achieve a unique distinction in 1946 when they became the first transatlantic arrivals to touch down at London's newly opened Heathrow Airport.

On the other side of the coin came the unfortunate *Bristol Brabazon*, a giant of an aircraft that was way ahead of its time and, consequently, doomed to failure. Sky-high development costs turned the *Brabazon* into a political disaster area and it was eventually scrapped in 1953, a victim of its own futuristic ambitions.

Progressive developments in aircraft design resulted in the introduction of several outstanding airliners that drew admiring glances wherever they flew. *Douglas DC-4s, 6s* and *7s*, the ultra-modern *'Super' Constellations* and the imposing, magnificent *Boeing Stratocruiser* to name but a few.

Flown by both Pan American and BOAC, the *Stratocruisers,* with their luxury fittings and lower-deck cocktail bar provided the most comfortable transatlantic crossing of its time and became great favourites with their many passengers.

The forward momentum of airliner development showed no signs of slowing down though and, in July 1950, another milestone passed beneath the wings of a *Vickers Viscount* flying in the colours of British European Airways.

With twenty six passengers on board, the *Viscount* flew from London to Paris powered by four Rolls Royce *Dart* Turboprop engines – the first aircraft ever to fly a scheduled passenger service using gas-turbine power. Setting new standards of speed, economy and comfort, the turboprop engine brought air travel to the brink of the jet age and, in doing so, sent aloft an aircraft that became known worldwide as *'The Whispering Giant'*.

This aircraft, the outstanding *Bristol Britannia*, was a stalwart among airliners and graced the airways for many years with its quiet, reassuring presence. The *'Brit'* holds a special place in my own affections, as the aircraft that carried me safely home after almost three years of military service in the Far East. British Eagle flew the charter and gave many of us our first taste of civilian airliners – a taste we found much to our liking after some of the more spartan flights we'd experienced with the Royal Air Force.

The *Britannia* also provided the stage for one of the more outrageous and hilarious incidents recorded in this book (see chapter 3).

Competition for customers began to hot up in the 1950s and BOAC, in an endeavour to attract more passengers, introduced second class travel. Extra seats were installed to offset the monetary loss, and tourist class legroom, consequently, became more restricted – an inconvenience that the majority of passengers were happy to put up with in the interests of thrift.

Jet Power

On May 2, 1952, thirty-six excited passengers boarded a *De-Havilland Comet 1* for a twenty-three hour flight to Johannesburg, South Africa. Incredibly, this would be almost ten hours quicker than any previous flight over the 6,700 mile route.

The *Comet* was a turbojet – the first jet airliner to enter the propeller-strewn field of commercial passenger aviation. It was the first of a dynasty of superplanes.

The Russian twin-jet *Tu-104* pipped the Americans into second place, but when the *Boeing 707* eventually rolled out of the hangar to send the United States into the jet age, it was to prove one of the most influential aircraft of all times. In 1959 Pan American's *707, Clipper Windward* established the first round-the-world passenger flight, proving at last that airliners were truly global. Another *707, City of Canberra*, flying for Qantas Empire Airways, inaugurated its first trans-Pacific flight in the same year by flying from Sydney to San Francisco

.

The clamour for the new jets was so great that the second-hand market in piston-engined airliners became distinctly overcrowded. Only one airline, Icelandair, resisted the lure of the big jets and advertised itself proudly and blatantly as the 'One and only non-jet airline servicing the North Atlantic.'

The 1960s marked an upward trend in airliner design, with the majority following the lead of the French *Caravelle* with its rear-mounted engines. The *DC-9* and *BAC-111* took to the skies, followed by the tri-jets in the form of the *Trident, Boeing 727* and the imposing Russian *Tupolev 154*. Britain's *VC10* led the field as the first long-range aircraft powered by four rear-mounted engines.

Two separate events in the field of commercial aviation were to quickly overshadow all other developments during this decade. The first would introduce an aircraft that would dwarf every other airliner in the skies and dominate the airways into the 1990s. The second would lead passenger-carrying airliners to the threshold of the space age.

In 1966, the Boeing company began construction work on a new airliner that would be capable of carrying up to five hundred passengers in total, spacious, comfort. On 9th February 1969, the *Boeing 747-100* took off on its maiden flight from Paine Airfield, Washington and flew into the wide blue yonder to gain immortality as the awesome *'Jumbo' Jet*. Any lingering doubts about the *747's* mighty strength were to be dispelled forever on the night of 24th June, 1982 (see chapter 4).

The *Jumbo* brought with it new realms of luxury, and banished forever the pre-conceived idea that all airliners would never be anything other than 'Narrow tubes crammed with people.' In the early days, before the economic recession forced airlines to make better use of its extra space, the *747's* first-class passengers could enjoy a glass of champagne and a turn around the upper deck dance floor before tucking into a gourmet meal. For those who preferred a more sedate form of in-flight entertainment there were brand new films to enjoy or music to suit all tastes, from Beethoven to the Beatles.

'Would you believe they played the same tunes coming over?'

A Pan American *Jumbo* made the first transatlantic foray in 1970, disembarking three hundred and sixty two passengers at

Heathrow on 22nd January. Fears that any aeroplane as big as the *Jumbo* would be commensurably noisy were quickly dispelled as the giant airliner descended for its landing approach. The *747's* Pratt and Whitney Turbofans proved to be far quieter than many smaller aero-engines in operation at the time, and proved that big does not always mean noisy.

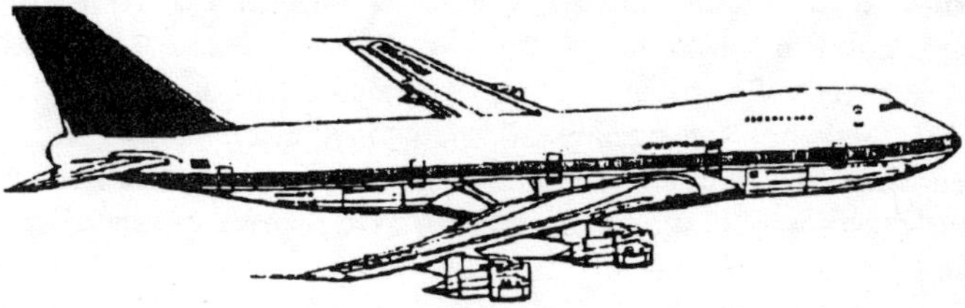

By the end of its first operational year, over one hundred *Jumbos* were in service with eighteen international airlines. Between them they had safely transported almost six million passengers over a distance exceeding fifteen billion miles – the *Jumbo* had arrived in style.

Individual airlines began to add their own innovations to the *747s* and an almost forgotten taste of luxury began to permeate the world of air travel once again.

Air India's *Jumbos*, glowingly advertised as 'Your Palace in the Sky' were all decorated with breathtaking scenes of ancient Indian folklore. Temple carvings adorned the cabin doorways and the splendidly named 'Maharajah' Lounge boasted a huge mural depicting the Ajanta Cave Frescoes, beautiful illustrations marking the religious events of the Lord Buddah.

Air Canada, on the other hand, chose to pay tribute to their country's other frontier transport service by decorating their aircraft in early Canadian railroad livery.

British Airways, also looking to the past for inspiration, introduced an Elizabethan Service on all its transatlantic flights and provided food and drink of the period to all its first and club class passengers. To complete the image they named ten of their *Jumbos* after famous people from the Elizabethan era. Sir Walter Raleigh and Sir Francis Drake competed with William Shakespeare and

Sir Richard Grenville for the affections of the passengers. Other airlines, likewise, took to naming their *Jumbos*. It didn't require a great deal of intense effort to link some of the aircraft with their country of origin either!

Bald Eagle, Lindberg, Kit Carson, Star of the Union and *Washington* could never, for instance, be associated with Lufthansa! *St Patrick, St Colmcille* and *St Kieran* could only be flying in Aer Lingus colours, whilst *Melbourne, Sydney and Canberra* graced the nose sections of Qantas aircraft. America's National Airline took the unusual step of naming all their fleet after serving stewardesses, an indication of the high regard in which they held their airgirls (chapter 3 takes a closer look at air stewardesses and their varied adventures).

The *747 Jumbo jet* is now a firmly established favourite with pilots and passengers alike and looks set to grace our skies for many years to come. British Airways showed clear intention of their future plans for the big jets when they placed an unprecedented four billion pound order for thirty-three of the latest *747-400* models in 1990. In addition, they negotiated an option to switch this order to an even bigger *'Jumbo Jumbo'* being planned by the Boeing company—an aircraft that would be capable of carrying over six hundred passengers.

Of all the passengers carried by the Jumbo jet, only one had the honour of riding on the outside! In 1977 the space shuttle, 'Enterprise' was carried aloft on the back of a 747 for pre-launch air tests and earned a new, if not suitably heroic, motto for the NASA space programme: 'Piggy-back to the stars'.

Supersonic Dream

In 1962 an agreement between the British and French governments to build a supersonic passenger carrying plane, led to the arrival of the sleek and graceful *Concorde*—the ultimate airliner.

On the 21st January, 1976 (11.40 GMT) two Concordes, one belonging to Air France, the other to British Airways, stood on their respective runways in Paris and London awaiting the completion of a thirty second countdown that would send them into the air simultaneously. The world's first supersonic passenger service was under way and air travel had entered another dimension.

Passengers can now travel between Great Britain and America at over twice the speed of sound in perfect comfort. Sumptuous lunches are served by stewardesses who are borne over ten miles in the time it takes them to finish pouring a glass of champagne.

To really appreciate the speed at which *Concorde* flies, take a look at the facts surrounding an unofficial 'race' in the 1970s between Britain's *Concorde* 002 and a *747* belonging to Air France. 002 took off from Boston, destination Paris, at exactly the same time as the *747* left Paris for Boston. 002 landed at Paris, spent over an hour on the ground taking on passengers and then took off again for the return trip. It overtook the *747*, still on its outward leg, and landed back at Boston eleven minutes ahead of the Air France aircraft!

Great emphasis on Concorde's speed has often led to disparaging and humorous comparisons. Prior to entering service it was used to convey various dignitaries on demonstration flights around the Bay of Biscay – a distance in excess of one thousand miles. Because it only took Concorde around an hour and a half to complete the journey these flights were cheekily referred to by flight crews as 'Trips around the Bay'.

Air travel is no longer restricted to the rich and privileged, nor is it the risky business it used to be in its infancy. Millions of ordinary people are now boarding aircraft as casually as they once jumped on trains and coaches, ensuring that airliners are now an essential part of everyday life. Unlike the golden days of early air transport, modern airliners are often taken for granted, rarely thought worthy of comment or even an upward glance as they pass overhead and are revered only by a small band of enthusiasts. Their history however, merits far more for these monarchs of the air.

The transformation from the deafening, oil-spraying bi-planes of the 1920s to the supersonic *Concorde* has taken less than eighty years—a feat that has no equal in engineering technology or human endeavour. The question facing passenger aviation as the century draws to a close has to be, "Are there any new frontiers left to conquer?"

The answer is, "Yes."

Space!

Plans for the development of the space shuttle as a fare-paying passenger carrier are already in hand and, who knows, in another eighty years, passengers enjoying a pre moon-landing drink will read of the inaugural shuttle service and marvel at how primitive it all used to be.

Of one thing we can all be certain. The same spirit of adventure, tempered by a unique humour, that sent airmen and airgirls aloft in the past will remain with those who fly in the future.

Their story is yet to come.

These are the stories of yesterday and today – dramatic, funny and inspiring.

Prepare for take-off...

Chapter 2

Tales from the Cockpit

So there I was – upside down with both engines on fire – nothing on the clock but the maker's name..."

"So there I was – on-board computer playing up, forcing me to actually FLY the darn thing – nothing on the menu but fresh salmon, oysters and caviar..."

Times, and the aeroplanes, may change but flyers never will. The stories they exchange over a few off-duty drinks will travel along the 'grapevine' and crop up time and again wherever aircrew meet for a convivial gathering. Some of the stories will be attributed to different characters or airlines, others will grow with the telling until they bear little resemblance to the original incident.

The tales in this chapter, to the best of my knowledge, are all true and accurate accounts of actual events.

Mysteries Beyond

Strange and mysterious incidents concerning airliners began to reach an astonished public as early as 1948 when a British *Tudor*, the *Star Tiger* vanished without trace over the Bermuda Triangle.

This notorious stretch of the Western Atlantic between Bermuda, Florida and Puerto Rico has long been associated with unknown forces and vanishing ships, but the loss of the *Star Tiger* sent fresh waves of unease through those who believed that UFOs or time warps were responsible for the disappearances.

The loss of the *Star Tiger* may or may not have been due to mysterious forces. Suffice to say that the more dramatic accounts of its disappearance failed to mention that it was last seen flying low to avoid strong headwinds. A sudden emergency would have given little chance for the crew to broadcast a mayday alert.

Although controversy surrounds the Bermuda Triangle mystery, other strange occurrences are not so easily brushed aside...

In 1954, a BOAC *'Monarch' Stratocruiser* flying high over Canada, came into contact with no less than seven UFOs. Passengers and crew witnessed a large, cigar shaped metallic object leading six smaller craft on a corresponding course with their aircraft. The strange machines accompanied the *Stratocruiser* for almost eighty miles, making no attempt to close with the aircraft or communicate in any way. The airliner's captain decided to radio for assistance and a fighter was scrambled to intercept the unidentified objects.

As the fighter closed on its target at maximum thrust, the UFO's accelerated with blinding speed and disappeared into the upper atmosphere. No rational explanation was ever found.

In America, the crew of a National Airlines *DC-4* bound for Washington spotted a circular, brilliant blue-white object hovering just below and to the west of their aircraft. The time was 3am, July 13th 1952.

As they continued to view the object, it suddenly started to climb towards them, stopping within a mile of their location at the same altitude. It kept pace with the *DC-4* for several miles, changing course only when the captain decided to switch on all the external aircraft lights in an attempt to communicate with it.

The UFO's response was immediate. It shot upwards at an estimated speed of 1,000mph and disappeared into space.

Eerie though these encounters were, the events surrounding the crash of an Eastern Airlines *L-1011 Tristar* airliner in 1972 were to result in several spine-tingling incidents that would seriously challenge the concept that there is no life after death.

Following the fatal crash of Flight 401 in the Florida Everglades, strange happenings began to occur on some of the other *L-1011s* of Eastern's fleet. Notably those fitted with spare parts from the wreck of Flight 401...

A stewardess, checking her cabin listings on one such aircraft, noticed an Eastern captain in uniform sitting in one of the passenger seats. The cabin was otherwise deserted. Thinking that he was returning from an outward flight, a regular occurrence, she approached him with a view to clarifying the situation.

The captain did not respond to her question and continued to stare fixedly ahead as though not aware of her presence. Worried, she called her own captain from the flight deck.

He came immediately but froze in his tracks when he caught sight of the silent figure.

"My god, it's Bob Loft," he said in disbelief.

Bob Loft was the pilot who had lost his life on Flight 401!

Before either could recover from their shock, Captain Bob Loft vanished in front of their eyes!

Second Officer, Don Repo, also killed in the *L-1011* disaster, began to appear in front of his former colleagues, even warning them of a potentially dangerous fault on one occasion. In his book, 'The Ghost of Flight 401', John Fuller relates the full, incredible story of the phantom airmen and the quest to establish contact with second officer Repo. The outcome is fascinating and deeply thought-provoking.

Airlines, naturally, are not keen to publicise events such as these and many witnesses are reluctant to relate their experiences through fear of ridicule. Great mysteries of the sea have fascinated millions over the years—The *Flying Dutchman*, sailing its ghostly course, The *Mary Celeste* floating peacefully on a calm sea with no sign of its crew, and many more.

Will generations to come shiver with delicious anticipation as strange and wondrous tales of the air are told and re-told in hushed tones around the firesides of dimly lit inns? Can we expect an ancient aviator to stoppeth one of three and hold him spellbound with a tale as gripping as the ancient mariner's?

The answer has to be, "Yes".

It would be unthinkable to believe otherwise.

The Black Sheep

During the early 1970s a 'go-slow' by air traffic controllers at America's J.F. Kennedy Airport resulted in lengthy delays and considerable frustration for flight crews and passengers alike. On this particular occasion, a long line of aircraft were wending their way, painfully slowly, towards the take-off point. It wasn't unusual for aircraft to be kept in the holding pattern for up to two hours waiting for clearance for take-off, and tempers, understandably, became a little frayed.

As the nose to tail procession crawled forward, the air traffic controller's voice cut in, advising the crews that the duty runway had been changed and would, subsequently, incur even further delays. For one of the pilots this proved the final straw. In a moment of sheer frustration he thumbed his transmit button and gave earthy vent to his feelings.

"Aw, s**t!" he swore, with great emphasis on the last word.

There was a long moment of silence before the controller's voice came back on the air.

"Which aircraft," he demanded in a slow New York drawl, "said 's**t'?"

There was another long pause while everybody waited for the miscreant to own up.

A transmit button clicked:

"Pan Am 201, tower, we didn't say s**t!"

"Speedbird 501. We didn't say s**t either."

"TWA 536 didn't say s**t!"

This went on for several minutes before the resigned controller cut in:

"Okay, fellers, that's enough s**t for one day. Let's get back to work."

The Ugly Duckling

The *Bristol Freighter* could never be described as a 'Lovely aeroplane' and anyone who has flown as a passenger in one will not be surprised at the nickname given to it by the troops in the far east during the 1960s...

The Bristol Frightener!

It was a short, squat little monster with a bulbous nose that opened sideways in two sections to allow cargo to be loaded. Nevertheless, it had its admirers and one such was a British pilot arriving proudly on the circuit at JFK Airport, New York.

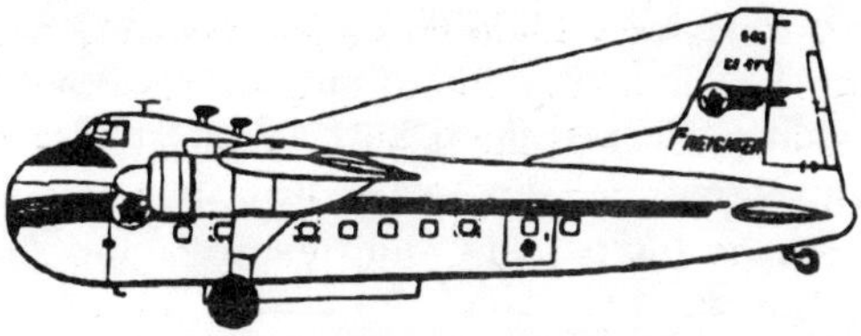

The Bristol 'Frightener'

The sight of the aircraft, closely resembling one of the bulldogs that Americans fondly associate with the British, drew astonished glances from all around. After the aircraft landed (a controlled crash as the troops unkindly referred to it) the controller could contain his curiosity no longer.

"Say, what kind of a ship is that, Captain?" he queried.

A very English voice, full of pride, provided the answer.

"This, Sir, is a *Bristol Freighter*. One of the finest examples of British aviation technology."

"The controller, with typical New York humour, replied:

"Gee, did you make it yourself?"

Passion Killer

The captain of a *VC10*, en-route from Los Angeles to Australia, had just been served his in-flight meal and was about to tuck in with relish when his chief steward arrived on the flight deck with news of a passenger confrontation.

"There's a lady wants to see you, skipper. Claims she's been grossly insulted by the crew," he informed his hungry captain.

Groaning inwardly at the unsavoury prospect of a domestic scene, he asked the chief steward to explain the situation fully.

A young Australian man had apparently been invited to sit alongside a flirtatious American lady and an excess of alcohol had led to what the steward referred to as "a fair old grope!"

As passion overtook them, so the language became very fruity indeed and, as there were women and children on board, the steward had taken the Australian to the back of the cabin for a word of caution.

"I told him that we'd received complaints from the other passengers and that this sort of behaviour would not be tolerated any longer," he related. "I warned him that a resumption of their disgraceful antics would force me to inform the captain."

The Australian had staggered back to inform his new-found lady love of the threat and she immediately demanded, in a very strident voice, to see the captain with regards to the 'gross insult' suffered at the hands of the chief steward.

Staring longingly at his fast-congealing meal, the captain instructed the steward to inform the lady that he would see her in fifteen minutes when he had finished eating, reasoning that this would also give her time to cool down. Thirty seconds later, a dishevelled chief steward re-appeared on the flight deck. Behind him could be heard the sounds of a frantic struggle and the raised voice of the indignant American lady. Enraged at the captain's seemingly indifferent attitude she had attempted to storm the flight deck single handed. Cabin staff had forcibly restrained her in the forward galley.

Acknowledging the futility of further delay, the captain climbed out of his seat, donned his uniform cap ("It adds dignity to the occasion.") and went out into the forward galley.

The sight of the inebriated woman was not a pretty one.

Lipstick was smeared liberally over her lower face and mascara was running free on the upper reaches. The captain, with grim dignity, asked if he could be of any assistance.

"Yeah – I've been grossly insulted by that bludger over there," she slurred, jerking a thumb in the direction of the chief steward.

"Madam, I do not believe that to be the case," replied the captain. "Furthermore, you have behaved in a disgraceful manner, your language has been disgusting and obscene and I will not tolerate it any longer. You will return to your seat and behave yourself for the remainder of the flight or I shall radio the authorities and ask them to off-load you in Honolulu."

The lady in question considered this statement for all of ten seconds before responding:

"Up yours, Jack. I'm going right back in there and I'm going to screw that feller in front of all the passengers and, what's more, when we arrive in Honolulu – I'm going to shoot you!"

With that she turned and stormed back to her seat.

Thinking quickly, the unruffled pilot informed his chief steward to turn off the cabin lights and if the lady couldn't restrain herself from carrying out the first part of her threat, he was to throw a blanket over the couple. She couldn't and he did!

All passion spent, the amorous couple were fast asleep when the *VC10* touched down at Honolulu, and it was decided that no charges would be made against them. They were allowed to continue their journey and caused no further problems. The wording of the Hawaiian duty officer's report of the incident was worth framing:

"Once they had had an intercourse they went fast asleep and were fast asleep right through the transit to Honolulu. We did not consider that, now that they had had-it-off, that there would be any further bother."

Word of the incident spread quickly along the grapevine and the airline fraternity lost no time in according the unfortunate captain a new title.'The fastest brothel-keeper in the west.'

The Trials and Tribulations of Captain Tommy Thompson

For Captain, Tommy Thompson, the slight jolt as the BOAC *749 'Connie'* touched down at Darwin heralded his first contact with Australia – land of opportunity and sunshine. He was looking forward to acquainting himself with the people and their culture.

He didn't have long to wait!

With the *'Connie'* safely in the hands of its relief crew, Tommy and his first officer made for the airfield mess for breakfast. Entering the dining hall they settled themselves at a table and waited patiently to be served.

Twenty minutes later they were still waiting.

Tommy, hungry and tired after his flight, decided to go into the kitchen to find out what the hold up was.

"If you'se is bloody staff, sport, you eat in the bleeding kitchen like everybody else," came the reply to his courteous enquiry.

With a note of resignation in his voice, Tommy summoned his co-pilot into the steamy kitchen and both men sat on a bench at a long, bare wooden table. The only other diner, an unshaven, very unkempt individual dressed only in a pair of greasy, knee-length shorts, ignored their polite, 'Good mornings.'

Two huge plates of steak, egg and chips were duly pushed under the noses of the two pilots and Tommy ventured to strike up a conversation with their Australian fellow diner by asking him to pass the salt.

A momentary silence followed the pilot's request, whilst the Australian struggled to swallow the food he'd been shovelling into his mouth. Finally, he addressed the British Captain with the following words:

"There ain't no slaves in Australia—get it yer bleedin' self!"

'Excuse me old chap, can I see the wine list?'

At the hotel in Darwin that evening, Tommy was all ready to forgive and forget his first encounter on Australian soil as he sat down for his evening meal. Service would, he felt, be much improved at this establishment.

Which, in retrospect, shows just how wrong even senior captains can be at times...

"My soup arrived, and a large mug of very strong tea was plonked down beside it," shuddered the pilot. "I told the waiter that I didn't take tea with dinner and asked for the wine list."

A look of considerable scorn appeared on the waiter's face and Tommy's cultural education took a step further as the indignant Australian gave vent to his feelings:

"What's wrong with the bleeding tea then? Are you some kind of a bleeding poofter, or what?"

Despite this disastrous start, Tommy became very fond of Australia and its people, regarding it as one of his favourite stopovers. He remembers with affection one particular trip when he was route clearing the late Nigel Perry (the pilot who flew Prime Minister, Neville Chamberlain to his notorious 'Peace in our time' meeting with Adolf Hitler).

"Nigel was a most delightful Irishman who was extremely proud of the fact that he once played cricket for the 'Gentlemen of Ireland'", recalled Tommy. "We were on the Singapore – Darwin leg of the flight and there was a hell of a storm raging. Lightning was flashing every couple of seconds and we were being bounced all over the sky. It didn't add to our peace of mind that we were flying over the Timor Sea either – it's full of sharks!"

Nigel had sat pensively in the co-pilot's seat, gazing meditatively out at the raging storm.

"I was wrestling with the controls when Nigel, who had never been to Australia, turned towards me," said Tommy. "In his lovely Irish brogue he said, 'You know, Tommy, I'm going to Australia with a completely open mind – but mind you, I'm a little bit prejudiced!'"

As it turned out, Nigel had the time of his life in Australia, being invited to sit with the MCC tour party during a test match at Sydney cricket ground. Tommy had secured free tickets by simply showing their pilots licences – a guarantee of preferential treatment in certain quarters in those far-off days.

Clipped Wings

During his long career, Tommy was given the opportunity to visit Grendon Underwood Prison, an establishment catering for violent criminals. This was of particular interest to Tommy, whose voluntary magisterial duties continue to this day.

"I was in a common room with several murderers and a couple of rapists," he recalled, "when one of the double murderers sidled up to me and asked what I did for a living.

On being informed that his visitor was a civil airline pilot flying for BOAC, the hardened offender looked at Tommy in envious amazement.

"Cor! That's a bloody cushy job and no mistake," he stated. "Lying in the sun all day with the birds."

"I tried to tell him it wasn't like that—well, not all the time anyway—but he wouldn't be convinced," laughed Tommy. With gruesome logic the prisoner offered his final opinion on the matter:

"Well, if I could've gotten a job like yours, I wouldn't be here now, would I?"

Ford Open Prison in Sussex provided a lighter setting for Tommy's next magisterial visit and it was here that he came face-to-face with the familiar figure of one of his ex-chief stewards.

"I remembered him very well from the late fifties when he led what became known as the 'Gold Rush' from BOAC," he explained. "A large number of our stewards suddenly left the company for pastures new when a gold smuggling ring between Hong Kong, India and Pakistan was broken by the police. They took the sensible decision and departed from aviation rather than risk long prison sentences should they ever return to those countries."

Tommy had been hailed with enthusiasm by his ex-chief steward.

"Hello, Skipper. What on earth are you doing here?" he called out as he rushed forward, smiling, to shake hands.

"More to the point," replied Tommy, "what are you doing here?"

"Nine years," came the laconic reply.

Captain Tommy Thompson was not always on the right side of justice or the authorities though...

"South Africa used to be the only place where crew members had to fill-in arrival forms," he remembered. "We all used to play games with them and they were usually returned with answers like 'Mum' for mother's name, 'Dad' for father's name or, 'Occasionally' for sex. On this particular occasion I thought I'd be extra clever by answering the question, 'Race' with, 'Human'," he grinned. "The immigration officer, who had no sense of humour at all, noticed this and asked me doggedly if I was African or European, even though it was plainly obvious where I came from."

Tommy made his first mistake.

"I'm a European, what are you?" he answered.

"Man, I'm a European as well," replied the official.

"Where were you born?" queried Tommy in a friendly tone.

"Right here, in Jo'burgh," came back the proud assertion.

Tommy made his last mistake.

"Then you must be an African," he informed the, by now, grim faced immigration officer.

It took three and a half hours for Tommy to clear customs.

"They squeezed my toothpaste and shaving cream out, cut up my soap, ransacked my baggage, strip-searched me inside and out. It was an experience I never want to go through again," winced the rueful pilot.

Arrival forms at Johannesburg, it was rumoured, were filled in correctly thereafter by cautious (Tommy prefers, 'Lily livered') flight crews.

"Where's the Fire?"

The following story illustrates clearly the rapid and dramatic change that took place in airport security following the first hijacking of an international airliner.

Prior to this frightening act of terrorism, very little in the way of protection existed for flight crews who suddenly found themselves confronted with an armed aggressor—as Captain, Tom

Wright found out to his cost as he prepared for take off from the West German Capital of Bonn...

"I was just about to start the *1-11's* first engine," he recalled, "when my stewardess came onto the flight deck and informed me that one of the male passengers had been seen concealing a revolver under his shirt. I immediately informed the tower that I had a firearms situation and requested assistance."

Five minutes later, a fire engine arrived!

"By this time, I'd told the passengers that we had a problem with one of the engines and take-off would be delayed," said Tom. "I left the aeroplane as casually as I could and went over to the fire engine crew to explain that I needed burly policemen, not firefighters, to deal with the problem at hand."

Three quarters of an hour later, after some desperate stalling by Tom, a little police Volkswagen *Beetle* could be seen making its unhurried way across the airfield.

'Yes, it's a big man with a big gun. Send reinforcements.'

"I took one look at this 'taskforce' that had been sent out, and decided that I would have to try to get everyone off the aircraft before things got out of hand," explained Tom. "I told the passengers that complications had arisen with the engine and that they would be required to return to the terminal building whilst repairs were carried out."

All the passengers, including the armed man, began to leave their seats in readiness for disembarkation.

"I grabbed hold of my stewardess and made sure we got off first," said Tom. "I rushed her over to the three policemen and instructed her to point out the hijacker as he came off."

The passengers filed slowly down the steps, unaware of the drama unfolding around them, and began to make their way back to the terminal building. As the armed suspect passed her, the stewardess quietly identified him to the three police officers who had been sent to deal with the situation.

"They moved quickly into the line of passengers and began working their way towards him," said Tom. "The next thing I knew, this chap was lifted bodily into the air with his arms pinned to his side and carted over to the police car. The revolver was removed from his waistband and he was unceremoniously bundled on to the back seat. The last I saw of any of them, they were trundling slowly back across the airfield."

With the danger over, Tom immediately re-boarded his mystified passengers and the rest of their journey to Berlin passed without further incident.

Two months later, Captain Tom Wright flew back into Bonn.

"During that short space of time, hijacking had hit the headlines with a vengeance," he recalled. "Everybody was shocked and appalled at this latest development in terrorism and, naturally, security had tightened up somewhat since my little adventure."

How much it had tightened up came as a bit of a shock to Tom, who had not forgotten his experience with the fire engine and police car.

"The place was surrounded by military forces and you couldn't move for armed police and soldiers," he recollected grimly. "The whole airport seemed to be bristling with weapons and fast-moving security vehicles. The changes that had taken place were almost beyond belief, and I couldn't help wondering what would have happened if our little incident had taken place two months later."

Fire engines were to figure prominently in one more adventure for Tom Wright and, again, he was not to be overly thrilled at their involvement...

"This was a flight just before my retirement," recalled the pilot. "I'd just taken off from Portugal when there was a tremendous *'crump'* from the vicinity of the undercarriage. It was obvious that something had happened to one or more of the tyres, so I made a request for the ground engineer to inspect the runway and make an assessment of the problem."

The engineer duly reported that, in his opinion, it was the nose wheel tyre tread that had broken away.

"I decided to carry on to London," said Tom, "but the weather wasn't exactly perfect for us. It was a very dark, bleak winter's night with low cloud. I briefed my senior steward that I'd declared a partial emergency and that there was a possibility that the nose wheel might collapse on landing."

Heathrow had been alerted and had given a priority clearance for Tom's flight on a cleared runway.

"We broke cloud at about 300ft," he estimated, "when the ground controller suddenly called for me to overshoot and go around again. We were at about 200ft at the time and I wasn't at all pleased about this instruction. However, I had no choice in the matter and climbed for another circuit."

After a short pause, the ground controller called through with an explanation for the aborted landing.

"He told me, rather sheepishly, that the fire engines on stand-by for my emergency had set off in pursuit of the wrong aircraft and were still on the runway as I was making my approach," said Tom. "I circled for another attempt and this time landed without incident."

As the aircraft taxied to its parking bay, it became apparent that the blown tyre tread had indeed caused extensive damage. One engine, the undercarriage and part of the flap mechanism received such a battering that they needed replacing altogether.

However, one bright moment was to emerge from this potentially dangerous incident and Tom Wright still remembers it as one of the highlights of his flying career.

"The passengers had disembarked and a whole bunch of airport officials had rushed on board to ensure everything was in order," he recalled. "They were all on the flight deck, rabbiting on about this, that and the other, when I heard the voice of one of my stewardesses coming from the back of the throng."

The stewardess, a petite and very pretty girl, was obviously in no mood for niceties, event though in the presence of officialdom.

"I could hear her shouting, 'Out of the way, come on, out of my way,' and then I caught sight of her, literally elbowing aside all these dignitaries as she forced her way into the cockpit. They were being shoved off balance, pushed against the sides and everything," laughed the pilot.

Tom watched in amazement as the little stewardess carved a swathe through the assembled hierarchy, until, at last, she stood in front of him.

"She threw her arms around me and said, 'Thank you, Captain Wright – thank you for getting us down safely.' Then she gave me a real smacker of a kiss right on the lips," he recalled with delight. "I thought that was a marvellous gesture and I must admit it made me feel a little bit special."

'Performed another heroic landing have we captain?'

Tom was only a few short months away from retirement when this incident occurred and it was, he hoped, his last near miss as a commercial airline pilot.

Unfortunately, it wasn't...

"I was flying a *707* back from Rome, getting ready for the descent into London," he explained. "We were at about 30,000ft when I suddenly heard the ground controller clear an aircraft at 33,000ft down through my level."

With a feeling of unease, Tom intuitively lent forward in his seat and peered up through the top of his front windscreen.

"As I looked up, I could see a *Trident 2* descending right on top of me – it couldn't have been more than a couple of yards distant," estimated the pilot. "I whipped out the autopilot and swung to starboard, out of his way."

The two aircraft missed each other by feet and the startled pilot of the *Trident* found himself flying alongside Tom's *707*.

"The captain was an ex-first officer of mine but the last thing either of us had on our minds was how nice it was to see each other," smiled Tom. "The poor old controller nearly had a coronary when I told him he'd just cleared a *Trident* down through my level, and that it had just tried to use me as a runway!"

The controller's confusion had arisen from a recent change of policy whereby the old alphabetical identification letters had been replaced by today's familiar numerical call signs.

For Captain Tom Wright, this frightening air-miss proved to be the last hair-raising adventure of a long and distinguished career. He went to ground, along with a surprising number of other ex-airline pilots, in Hampshire's peaceful, crisis-free, New Forest.

The Incredible Tales of Johnny Tempest*

Every so often, a larger than life character of great presence will arrive on the world stage of passenger aviation, enriching the lives of all who are lucky, or unlucky, enough to be drawn into their charismatic force field. One such character was Captain Johnny Tempest* whose exploits will surely survive forever in the annals of aviation folklore.

Johnny was a British pilot, a big, burly man with a large, piratical black beard that looked oddly out of place on some of the more sophisticated aircraft he flew in the latter part of his varied career. The first recorded episode highlighting his wonderfully eccentric behaviour however, took place on a *Dragon Rapide* biplane in the early fifties. The *Rapide* was a short-haul aircraft, ideal for the Aberdeen–Orkney flight that Johnny was about to undertake on this particular occasion. It could only accommodate a small number of passengers.

Prior to their arrival, Johnny had donned a Scottish cape and fearsome looking clan bonnet and slipped furtively aboard the *Rapide*, taking up one of the rearmost seats near the cabin door. There he remained until the unsuspecting passengers came on board and settled themselves to patiently await the arrival of their pilot.

As the minutes ticked by, Johnny took to studying his watch with increasing regularity and growling fiercely at the delay.

"Five more minutes," he suddenly bellowed, "and if he hasn't turned up by then, I'm going to fly this thing myself."

As the minutes ticked agonizingly by, apprehension amongst the passengers increase-drapidly. Everyone took to staring out of the cabin windows, looking vainly for signs of the missing pilot. Exactly five minutes later, Johnny rose to his feet and, with terrible deliberation, slammed the cabin door shut.

'That's it, I'll fly the bloody thing!'

"That's it," he informed his now frenzied companions, "I'll fly the bloody thing."

With this, he stormed into the cockpit, started the engines and took off!

Far from receiving furious complaints about their captain's outrageous behaviour, the airline found, to their amazement, that he had achieved celebrity status. Booking clerks began taking calls from passengers who asked specifically to be placed on one of Johnny's flights.

A legend was born!

During the heyday of the *Vickers Viking* airliners, it became company policy for captains to ensure their passengers were kept suitably entertained whilst in-flight. This involved the captain making frequent visits to the cabin and chatting sociably with the customers.

'Keep the passengers amused' was how part of the written instructions ran.

Word had apparently reached the ears of the airline's moguls that Johnny was not paying sufficient attention to this instruction and, consequently, his passengers were not being 'amused'.

A formal letter was sent to the errant captain, pointing out his shortcomings and demanding that he rectify the situation immediately.

On his next flight, prior to take off, Captain Johnny Tempest emerged from his cockpit in full dress uniform and addressed his complement of passengers.

"Good morning, ladies and gentlemen. May I have your attention please. I am Captain Tempest and it is my duty to inform you that I have been disciplined by the company for not amusing my passengers."

So saying, he produced a penny whistle from the inside pocket of his uniform jacket and proceeded to play a faultless rendition of, 'She'll be coming round the mountain' to his captive audience.

At the end of his solo performance, Johnny replaced the tiny instrument back in his pocket and, with a little bow, said:

"Ladies and gentlemen, I trust you are suitably amused."

With this, he re-entered the cockpit and was not seen again for the rest of the flight.

'Can my lad request 'Runaway Train', by Captain Tempest?'

There was never any doubt in the minds of Johnny's crew that he was the absolute master on any of the aircraft he commanded. One of his rulings, strictly enforced, concerned the presence of cabin staff on the flight deck and any steward or stewardess foolish enough to encroach on his domain without being summoned risked appalling reprisals.

Johnny's chief steward on board a routine European flight had responded immediately to one such summons and presented himself promptly on the flight deck. With a regal air, the pilot had handed him a flight information bulletin that he had consented to make out for the amusement of his passengers. These bulletins contained information about height, speed, notable landmarks, estimated time of arrival at destination and any other details considered of interest. The chief steward withdrew quietly and the information sheet was passed among the passengers. Within minutes, confusion and alarm spread through the cabin and the steward was hastily called to explain the contents of the offending bulletin.

"Steward. This says we're landing at Hamburg in half an hour," complained a well dressed spokesman for the agitated passengers. "Yet we're all booked for Copenhagen. Please can you go and ask your captain to explain what's happening?"

The steward paled visibly.

"I'm sorry, sir but I'm not allowed on the flight deck unless I'm called," he replied apologetically.

A scene of utter chaos ensued, with everybody shouting at once and demanding an official explanation for their wrongly-routed flight.

In the midst of all this excitement, the cockpit door opened and the imposing figure of Captain Johnny Tempest appeared– a look of stern reproach on his bearded face.

"What on earth is going on here?" he demanded, singling out the spokesman who had made the first complaint.

"You've written on this form," stuttered the apoplectic passenger, "that you're going to Hamburg, yet we're all booked for Copenhagen. We want to know what's going on."

The burly captain deliberated this outburst for some time, apparently giving the matter long and serious consideration. Eventually, he gave a long sigh and, with a note of resignation in his voice, addressed the worried throng.

"Oh, all right then. Flying's such a boring business anyway. If you want to go to Copenhagen, we'll go to Copenhagen."

With this, he re-entered the cockpit and flew on to Copenhagen.

Where, had the latest victim of Johnny's humour but known it, they were going from the outset!

The following, final account of Johnny Tempest's mid-air antics will probably bring smiles of recognition from airmen everywhere. The same prank has been attributed to dozens of pilots in the RAF, and usually occurred on troop-carrying aircraft. This tale, however, concerns the first, fully authenticated incident that I have ever come across involving a civilian airliner.

Johnny had progressed to the captaincy of a *Trident 3* at the time and this aircraft had a small, very exclusive first class compartment set at the front of the cabin, behind the cockpit. The well-heeled occupants of this compartment had settled down with their in-flight drinks and were in the process of either reading the 'Times' or studying various business documents, when the flight deck door opened and the bulky frame of Captain Johnny Tempest could be seen backing out into the first class area.

In both hands he was trailing two pieces of string that he carefully unravelled as he backed into line with the first row of passengers.

"Excuse me, sir," he addressed the well-groomed businessman sitting in the right hand aisle seat, "I wonder if you'd be so kind as to hold on to this for me and hold the aircraft steady while I nip down to the toilet."

Turning to an apprehensive-looking man in the left hand aisle seat, Johnny made the same request.

"I'm much obliged, gentlemen," he said gravely. "Now if you just keep the string taut, that should hold the control column steady."

When he returned a few minutes later, Johnny was wickedly gratified to see both his 'co-pilots' sweating freely as they strove desperately to maintain a steady pressure on the two pieces of string. The rest of the passengers, displaying all the symptoms of a mouse confronted by a snake, were staring, mesmerized, at their two frantic companions.

Johnny Tempest, captain extraordinary, had struck again!

Airmen will always find time for a yarn and, more often than not, are quite happy to divulge their own embarrassing adventures to a willing listener. They invariably prefer to recall the humorous moments and will even add a touch of comedy to the most frightening incident, providing everyone came out of it in one piece.

Computers, some say, will eventually replace every member of the flight deck crew. Perhaps they will.

One thing's certain though.

They'll never have the ability to tell a good story.

Chapter 3

Tea, Coffee... Paper Bags?

In March 1930, a letter written by a pretty and far-sighted young lady by the name of Ellen Church dropped through the letter box of America's United Airlines. Ellen, a registered nurse and licensed private pilot, suggested that the airline would benefit enormously if it employed suitably qualified ladies to act as aircraft cabin attendants – ladies, in fact, like herself.

United's moguls were taken aback by the idea of women flying as crew members, but were also quick to appreciate the possible commercial value of such a venture. Ellen was duly appointed and immediately charged with the task of selecting seven other girls to join United's expanding fleet.

Applicants were carefully vetted with emphasis being placed on their nursing experience, age and stature. Twenty-five was decreed the maximum age limit – it would require the resilience of youth to withstand the lengthy, often arduous flights that were being undertaken at the time. In addition, a petite 5ft 4in. restriction on the girls height was considered a necessity to avoid permanent headaches through collision with the low cabin roof.

Two months later, on 15th May, 1930, Ellen Church greeted her first eleven passengers on board a *Boeing 80A* for an interstate flight from Oakland, California to Cheyenne, Wyoming – a five-stage journey that took almost 24 hours to complete. As part of her duties, she had already cleaned the cabin from top to bottom, helped to push the aircraft out of the hangar and wielded a re-fuelling hose to fill the tanks prior to take off. Tough going for a slip of a girl like Ellen, yet one other burden was to fall heavily on the shoulders of both her and her fellow hostesses – resentment. On a grand scale!

The outcry that greeted the Royal Navy's decision to send WRENS to sea in 1990 merely echoed the clamour that arose when Ellen's young pioneers were accepted for flying duties in 1930. Not only did they face a wave of hostility from some of the men they were to fly with, but United Airlines offices were swamped with letters of protest from outraged pilot's wives demanding the girls dismissal forthwith.

Strength of character, cheerful optimism and sheer guts saw the hostesses win the day. Flying over a hundred hours a month in unheated, unpressurised aircraft, they quickly won praise from pilots and passengers alike for their unstinting efforts. United Airlines decided that they would remain at all costs and Ellen Church's magnificent seven led the way in setting a tradition of care, compassion and courage that became the hallmark of air stewardesses throughout the World. Alongside their male counterparts, the air stewards, they continue to symbolise the very best in passenger transportation service. Their stories are legion. Dramatic, hilarious, always rivetting. These are some of them.

Tit For Tat

A Bristol *Brittania* airliner, carrying immigrant passengers towards a new life in the British Isles, droned sedately through the night sky, its pilgrim journey not quite half over. The scene was one of peace and tranquillity – on the outside. The turbulence was confined to the passenger cabin!

Excited and emotionally charged at the prospect of life in a new country, the virile young passengers were presenting major problems for the Chief Steward.

"It was almost like an orgy," he recalled with some awe. "We had our hands full trying to keep some of those youngsters from venting their passion on board the aeroplane."

In desperation, he decided that the women would occupy the front end of the aircraft whilst the men cooled off in the rear.

"I took charge of the women, but I knew I'd have hell's own job trying to keep them amused for the rest of the flight," he said.

Salvation came in the form of a pen. Not just any old pen, but a highly valued airline pen with the company logo emblazoned richly along its streamlined barrel.

"At that time our pens were very much sought-after souvenirs," explained the Chief Steward. "Wherever we went in the world, everyone would be chasing us for one. Bell-hops, ground crew, passengers – we even used to get beggars asking for them instead of cash."

The women in his charge had been no exception, and he'd been pestered throughout the flight, ("Well, during the pauses between passionate clinches anyway!") with requests for his own company pen.

"I suddenly saw the answer to my problems," grinned the steward. "I would organize a competition with one of our pens as a prize for the winner."

That the idea was a runaway success, there was little doubt. The squeals of delight and beaming, enthusiastic smiles attested to that. The steward's inspirational brainwave, however, stopped short of an idea for the type of competition to run.

"I couldn't for the life of me think of anything sensible," he said. "The girls were getting a bit noisy and I was desperate to come up with something in a hurry. They were a very happy-go-lucky crowd and, judging by their earlier antics, certainly not prudes, so I came up with the only thing I could think of – a big tits competition!"

A momentary silence followed this inspired suggestion and, for one awful moment, the Chief Steward had visions of his much-prized job flying out of the window to vanish in the slipstream of the Britannia's four Bristol *Proteus* engines.

"The next thing I knew, the air was filled with discarded blouses and bras of all shapes and sizes," laughed the steward. "It was an amazing sight to behold, believe me. The girls were roaring with laughter – I expect my eyes looked as though they were on stalks."

Quickly choosing a likely candidate, the enterprising steward announced her the winner and, with great ceremony, presented her with the coveted pen. As a form of in-flight entertainment, it proved unbeatable, and the rest of the flight passed off peacefully.

It wasn't until the following week that retribution caught up with the Chief Steward.

"I was summoned to the manager's office and received the rollicking of my life," he grimaced. "They'd been sent a letter of complaint from one of the ladies on the flight. Not, you understand, complaining about the competition, but about the fact that she hadn't been declared the winner!"

In her letter, the young lady had informed the airline's moguls that she had been comparing the size of her boobs to those of her friend, Miranda (the winning contestant) and they were definitely bigger. In view of this result she felt that it would be only fair for the airline to send her a pen as well!

"I was well and truly carpeted by the airline, but not for running the competition," explained the perplexed chief steward. "They disciplined me for misappropriation of airline property. In other words, for giving away a company pen without permission!"

And talking of boobs...

Rashly Speaking

One of the hostesses on a *DC4* to Perth became aware, somewhere over the Nullarbor, that her chest was itchy. She went into the toilet and, upon unfastening her top uniform button and examining herself in the mirror, she was horrified to see the skin on her chest was covered with an angry red rash. She called her co-hostess in to have a look and suggested they go through the waybill to ascertain whether a doctor was on board who could diagnose the rash and tell if it was contagious.

Much to their delight they discovered a doctor sitting in seat 4A.

The 'non afflicted' one hurried down and approached him apologetically.

"Doctor," she said quietly, not wishing to alarm the other passengers, "would you mind coming with me?" She gently tugged at his arm, took his drink tray from him and propelled him down to the toilet.

"There's something we'd like you to look at," she said as she opened the toilet door to reveal her colleague stripped to the waist.

She pushed the doctor inside and shut the door.

"We're sorry to disturb you," the girl said, "but we thought you might be able to identify this rash."

She pushed her naked chest closer to the doctor who cowered back against the closed door, his face taking on a mottled look which almost matched the rash.

"You are a doctor, aren't you?" the girl enquired, "We looked you up on the waybill."

"Yes I am," stuttered the poor fellow, "but I'm a doctor of music!"

(From 'Up Here and Down There' by Nan Witcomb, July 1986 (Australia)).

"One Small Man for a Step"

(With apologies to astronaut, Neil Armstrong).

Following an overnight stop at Naples, a British Island Airways captain was carrying out his pre-flight 'walk around' checks on a *McDonnell Douglas 80*—an aircraft that had only just been delivered to the airline. Passing along the rear fuselage he noticed that the back passenger steps were still closed up and called across to one of his stewardesses.

"Julie, see if you can find an engineer to open up these steps before we have all our passengers trooping up the crew entrance."

In the manner of all good potential disasters, he had called on the one girl who had recently completed her conversion course on the *MD80* aeroplane and had, as part of the training, been instructed in the art of opening the back steps. Eager to show off her newly acquired skills she confidently breezed up to her captain's side.

"No need for that, captain, I can do that for you," she said brightly.

Dubious about allowing his slightly-built stewardess to manhandle the awkward looking steps, the pilot hesitated momentarily. However, there were no engineers in sight and, looking towards the terminal building, he could see the passengers approaching the aircraft.

"Okay, Julie, but watch what you're doing – don't hurt yourself," he warned as he moved off to complete his checks.

Delighted at being given the opportunity to display her newfound expertise, the stewardess stepped smartly up to the steps and stretched up to reach the release handle. Before she could lay hands on the door release, however, she was startled by a cry of Italian protest and found herself being bundled gently but firmly away from the steps.

"No! No! Issa no job for the beautiful lady. I will do this for you," enthused the gallant Neapolitan baggage handler who had intervened in what he took to be the stewardess's dire plight. Unable to stop him in time, Julie could only look on in horrified amazement as the little Italian, with half his attention still on the attractive English girl, leapt deftly up and pulled the protruding handle – the wrong protruding handle!

The effect was instantaneous and spectacular. With a glorious WHOOSH! of released energy, the entire contents of the emergency fire extinguishers sprayed upwards and outwards in an all-enveloping cascade of white foam.

The astonished passengers waiting to board the aircraft could only marvel at the demented antics of the frantic Italian as he danced around in anguish at the results of his noble, but misguided, gallantry.

Julie, with as much dignity as she could muster, rejoined her colleagues and spent the rest of the flight home averting the withering glare of her indignant captain. It was the first, and last, time that she was ever to be heard volunteering to open up the back steps!

"Shut That Door"

With a slightly heavier jolt than usual, an inbound *BAC 111* touched down at Gatwick Airport and began its long roll down the runway.

The aircraft's number two stewardess, 'Little Carol' Samuels, shot a quick, intuitive glance towards the over-wing exit door—just in time to see it jump off its hinges and fall inwards!

Quickly releasing her seat belt, she leapt dramatically across the aisle in a desperate bid to prevent the falling door inflicting any injuries to the passengers sitting nearby.

"I just managed to get my shoulder under it before it came crashing down," said the stewardess. "I struggled like mad to tilt it back, but couldn't quite do it. I just had to stand there, looking like a poor man's Supergirl and support it as we trundled down the runway."

When the aircraft finally rolled to a halt and reinforcements arrived to relieve the wilting stewardess of her burden, the assembled passengers treated her to a spontaneous round of applause and a rousing cheer. Beaming with pleasure, the blushing stewardess gave a mock curtsy and dashed hurriedly to her disembarkation station. Acts of derring-do are not considered by airlines to be sufficient reason to neglect normal duties!

One of the nicer sides to flying for a living is the opportunity to sometimes be able to repay a little of the debt owed to a loved one and, as a result of her quick thinking actions on board the

BAC 111, Carol Samuels was allowed to book her Dad on a 'Jolly' (free flight) as a reward for her initiative.

"I'd always wanted to do something for dad, to show him how much I really appreciated everything he'd done for me in my life," said Carol. "When the chance came to book him on a flight, I jumped at the offer. It was to be my last flight with the airline and to have my dad on board would be the 'icing on the cake' as far as I was concerned."

The day dawned and a very wary dad arrived at the airport, immaculately dressed and clutching a very smart pilot's bag – a present from his daughter.

"To tell the truth, dad was a little bit scared of flying," recalled Carol, "but when he found out that he was to sit on the flight deck, behind the captain and first officer, he was thrilled to bits. They were really great with him during the flight, explaining how everything worked and generally putting his mind at rest."

With a full complement of passengers to attend to, Carol found little time to think of anything but the next order – until midway through the flight.

"I was serving drinks about halfway down the cabin," recalled the stewardess, "I saw the flight deck door open out of the corner of my eye but didn't give it a lot of thought until I heard my dad's voice. When I looked up, there he was, complete with pilot's bag, parading grandly down the aircraft talking to the passengers."

With a slight feeling of shock, the amazed stewardess could only stare in wonder as her dad progressed steadily down the cabin. His jovial voice reached out to every passenger on board.

"Good morning. Good morning. Are you enjoying the flight? That's my daughter over there – it's her last flight today."

"It was obvious that he was enjoying every minute of his 'jolly' and he seemed to be really proud of me," said Carol with affection, "I felt a little bit special about that."

It wasn't the last time that the distinguished figure was to emerge from the flight deck to extol the virtues of his daughter either.

"If he came out of that cockpit once, he came out a dozen times," laughed Carol. "I don't know who the passengers thought he was, but if any of them thought he was the pilot, they must have been getting extremely worried at the amount of time he was spending away from the controls."

The life and Times of a High Flying Pearl Diver (circa 1945)

Eager to embark on a career amongst the clouds, 17 year old Bill Bunn presented himself proudly at the gates of Whitchurch Airfield in Bristol to begin training as an air steward for BOAC. The year was 1945 and the Second World War had just ended.

"I don't quite know what I expected to come first in my training programme," said Bill, "but it certainly wasn't to be shown a coke burning stove in a wooden staff canteen and told to clean it. Surely there couldn't be stoves on any of the aircraft I'd be flying in – or could there?"

Having completed his first task as a steward and proven himself a skilled and diligent stove cleaner, Bill was promoted to potatoes.

"They showed me this potato mountain and a huge milk churn," he chuckled, "'Fill the churn with spuds,' they ordered. Easy enough, I thought, chucking in handfuls at a time. 'Peeled,' they yelled – Not so easy after all."

Long and sustained periods of dishwashing duties followed Bill's culinary training, interspersed with trips out in the mobile canteen to sell refreshments to the hangar workers.

"We had to phone up the M.T. (Motor Transport) section to ask for a driver every time we went out, which was a bit frustrating for me and my pal," recalled Bill. "Being 17 and brash with it, we talked one of the drivers into teaching us to drive – highly unofficial, but an arrangement that suited both parties." This state of affairs lasted until the two lads were reported by an aggrieved and badly frightened pedestrian and 'grounded'.

Temptation in the form of a brand new Ford V8 giant mobile canteen proved too much for the two stewards and, as punishment for taking it for a joyride, they found themselves exiled to the Airways Terminal at Victoria, London. It was here that they were introduced to the pleasures of *'Pearl diving.'*

"Pearl diving was the kitchen name for dish washing in enormous sinks," explained Bill. "By the end of our punishment period, we were both experts on the subject."

A spell at Bournemouth's Hurn Airport followed, but the duties remained the same. Bill Bunn had yet to get his feet off the ground as a bona fide flying air steward.

"After a spell at Hurn, I was suddenly whisked away and deposited back at Whitchurch Airfield," he recalled with amusement. "They marched me up to this beautiful aeroplane and told me that I would be working it to Hurn in a couple of hours and then out to Cairo, via Lisbon, the following day. The aircraft was a *DC3*—the legendary *Dakota*."

The following morning found Bill back at Hurn Airport, waiting to greet his first passengers. The first leg of the journey, to Lisbon, would take them over the Bay of Biscay, a notoriously cold seven and a half hour flight.

"My first job before take-off was to dress every passenger in a flying suit and fur-lined boots. I made sure there was a spare set tucked away for myself because I'd been warned that every time a steward had the temerity to complain to his captain about the lack of warmth in his working area, he would be dismissed with the suggestion that he, 'put a bloody flying suit and boots on then!' I don't suppose we'll ever see the sight of a muffled, flying-suit clad steward serving tea to a cabin full of like attired passengers again."

After night stopping at Lisbon, the *DC3* flew down the West African coast to Accra, where a welcome three days off at a rest house provided the 17 year-old steward with his first taste of pampered luxury.

"All our meals were laid on, a personal servant allocated to every crew member and our laundry washed and ironed—all for sixpence a day," marvelled Bill.

The return flight to Hurn Airport marked the end of Bill Bunn's first trip. It had taken 21 days to fly to Cairo and back in the *DC3*— an adventure that very few 17 year old's are ever likely to experience. As Bill would describe it in his own inimitable style: "Pearl diver to cloud-hopper in one easy lesson."

Judy's Story

Early on the morning of Tuesday, 14th April 1964, I left Adelaide on flight 215 for Melbourne. One of our normal flight patterns was flights 215/216 ADL/MEL/ADL; this operated daily, and gave us about 3.5 hours in Melbourne to ring family, friends and have lunch prior to the 1pm departure of flight 216.

On this particular day, I had actually requested this flight pattern, as I had friends travelling to Melbourne on flight 215. The other hostess with me was Margaret Harper who had recently graduated.

At 12.30pm we boarded our *DC6B* aircraft VH-INA to prepare the cabin and buffet for our luncheon flight back to Adelaide. We had fifty-seven passengers on the flight, made up of approximately twenty First Class and the remainder Economy Class. Our passengers boarded, were equipped with reading matter, and Margaret and I then sat down for take-off. We had only been airborne for about two minutes when the aircraft shook violently and gave a severe lurch. The sensation was similar to a car hitting a deep ditch. Immediately, I saw the starboard side windows being doused with thick, black oil; not waiting for any 'six bells', I headed for the cockpit.

The crew were all working like one-armed paper hangers. Captain Keith Hants was on the radio, F/O Bob Gordon endeavouring to maintain a steady hold on the aircraft, and F/E Bert Clarke had his instrument panel lit up like a Christmas tree. Keith told me to get on the PA and inform the passengers that we had an emergency, to continue to observe the No Smoking and Fasten Sea Belt signs, and that he would speak to them in a few minutes time after he had discussed our situation with Ground Control.

Our situation basically was this: On take-off the propeller on the No. 3 engine had split and flown off, dragging the engine out of its mountings. The engine was left dangling down in front of the wing. The propeller, (now in several pieces) and parts of the engine, landed in back yards in Essendon; luckily no one on the ground was injured.

We flew out over Port Phillip Bay where Keith dumped most of our fuel, and we circled around the bay area so that if the engine did drop off, at least it would fall in a safe place!

'Shall I serve drinks or will we be down soon?'

In the cabin there was no real panic among our passengers, although it would be fair to say many were obviously frightened over our predicament. One lady started to cry rather loudly, but her husband gave her a quick backhander, and she was then content to just whimper quietly for the next hour. Another passenger indicated that he felt that there was no excuse for us not to proceed with serving bar and lunch, and yet another settled down to write out his will!

After we had been airborne for forty minutes, a *DC3* containing Captain Peter Gibbes and DCA officials flew alongside our aircraft inspecting the damage with binoculars. It was an incredible sight, seeing the other aircraft flying so close to ours; we could clearly see the people on board the *DC3,* and it gave one a rather warm feeling to know that these and many other people on the ground were really concerned about our safety, and were trying to help us in every possible way.

The decision was made, that any attempt to land whilst the engine was still hanging down lower than the undercarriage would be fatal. The fire risk alone was tremendous. Somehow we had to get rid of the offending engine. To this end, Keith commenced a 'shallow dive – sharp pull out' procedure to try to shake the engine off. These manoeuvres felt quite violent in the cabin, particularly as Margaret and I were, at this stage, demonstrating the ditching position to our passengers. The increased G-force caused by the above manoeuvre had us on the floor several times.

We were flying at about 1400 feet, and running very low on fuel when we finally rid ourselves of the engine. We headed straight back to Essendon. Full-scale emergency units were on hand at the airport, but thanks to Keith's skill, which was wonderfully supported by Bob and Bert, we made a smooth, safe landing. We had been in the air just under two hours.

Several amusing incidents came out of the above story. One of our passengers was a Dutch lady, who had just arrived in the country and spoke no English at all. We had not been informed of this prior to the flight, and I did not become aware of the problem. When I spoke to her regarding emergency procedures and ditching position, she smiled and nodded her head as if she understood me perfectly. After our arrival back at Essendon, she was taken in hand by an interpreter who asked her if she was all right. She replied that she was fine; that she had had a lovely flight, and that she couldn't get over how much Adelaide Airport looked the same as Melbourne Airport! She had no idea that she was back where she had started from. She had not understood one word said by the crew during the flight; she had not realised that anything was amiss. Innocence was bliss! She did go on to say, however, that she did think that we Australians were rather funny the way we sat for landing! No doubt the dear lady was quite surprised to find out later, when she flew on to Adelaide, that it is not normal practice to take up full brace position for every landing!

It was also reported that when news of the emergency was heard at Swanston Street, Miss Kit Clark, our Hostess Superintendent, immediately jumped into her car and headed for the Airport. As she approached Essendon, she was confronted by the police road blocks which were only permitting fire engines, ambulances and other authorised people through. The officer on the road block was really doing his job well, and there was no way that he was going to let her pass.

Miss Clark was adamant that she was going to get through; she informed him that she was the Hostess Superintendent and therefore entitled to pass. To this the officer supposedly replied, 'Yeah, and I'm Mother Goose'. I'm pleased to say that right won out, and Miss Clark was there to meet Margaret and I when we landed.

While our drama was going on, the airport was completely closed to all traffic. Meanwhile, an *Electra* was flying to Melbourne from Sydney. The captain was not aware of the situation at Essendon and was starting to build up his own problems. A short way out of Sydney, one of the engines on the *Electra* failed, and halfway down the track, a second engine failed. He radioed through to Melbourne requesting immediate clearance for landing on arrival, and was most surprised when he was told to clear out into a holding area or return to Sydney because there was another aircraft in the air with much more trouble than he had. He related next day, that compared to the problems which he had, he decided that if someone was in worse shape, they must have been "coming up from Tasmania in a *DC3*, and were rowing it!"

The Lockheed Electra

One small point, which I would also like to relate concerning this incident, is about the emergency drill. We all waded through our manuals religiously whenever we had a check coming up, and mostly ignored them for the rest of the time. However, the moment that the propeller parted company with the engine and the oil started to spray, it was as if someone had opened the manual at the *DC6B* Emergency Procedures page in front of my eyes, and it was all there for total recall. It proved to me, that if something important is learnt, it may lie dormant in a back corner of the brain for quite a long time, but it will jump forward when needed.

Our passengers were a great group of people that day; not once did anyone question our instructions to them, and two gentlemen with World War II RAAF experience, offered to assist in the cockpit if needed. After a successful landing was completed, the whole cabin broke into warm, spontaneous applause. I don't know to this day whether or not the crew in the cockpit heard it, but I hope they did. They deserved it!

(From 'Up here and Down There' Nan Witcomb, 1986. 'Judy's Story' re-printed with the permission of Judy (Murphy) Davis. 1990 Australia).

Birds of a Feather

Following a pleasant, trouble-free flight out to the Greek island of Kos, the crew of a *Boeing 757* were looking forward to an equally enjoyable return trip to Gatwick. With a full complement of relaxed and cheerful passengers, the cabin crew were anticipating a busy but happy home run.

The clear night sky beckoned enticingly as the *757* taxied out to the runway in readiness for take-off. Nothing, it seemed, could halt its majestic progress— until the captain aborted the take-off!

Puzzled at the delay, the passengers looked to the cabin crew for an explanation. Equally baffled, the stewardesses could only offer reassurance as they waited for word from the flight-deck. A second attempt to take-off was also aborted, and word came through that the problem was a flock of birds on and around the runway.

'We could be in real trouble if it's the mating season!'

One or two passengers, unaware of the perils of a bird strike, laughed incredulously at the thought of a technological marvel such as the *757* being grounded by a few birds. The fact remained though, that until the flock was dispersed, they weren't going anywhere. Stewardess, Wendy Walker takes up the story...

"They sent a landrover out to try and scare the birds away, but they wouldn't budge," she laughed. "They were racing up and down the runway, setting off explosions, blowing horns and goodness knows what else—it was like World War Three out there."

With the exception of a few faint-hearted birds, the flock merely gazed with interest at the landrover and, with 'Heard it all before' looks, stayed exactly where they were.

"The Captain had no option other than to wait for sun-up, when the birds would leave of their own accord," said Wendy. "There was no doubt that he'd made the correct decision because the pilot of an inbound aircraft reported to the tower that the birds were indeed a potentially dangerous hazard. Luckily, the passengers took it all in good part and we had no trouble at all from them."

The *757* finally rolled down the runway shortly after sun-up and arrived back at Gatwick without further mishap. The number one stewardess made the customary tannoy announcement, thanking the passengers for flying with them and apologising for the unfortunate delay caused by the flock of birds.

"She started to say the final spiel, which always included the names of the captain and first officer," grinned Wendy, "but as soon as she got the first part of the sentence out the passengers began roaring with laughter. They were whistling and shouting—you couldn't hear a word the poor old number one was saying."

Considering the experience they'd all shared on Kos, it was hardly surprising that the stewardess's landing speech met with such devastating ribaldry.

"Ladies and gentlemen, on behalf of your crew, Captain PECK and First Officer CROW...!"

The happy demeanour of all the passengers on board the grounded *757* made life a lot easier for Wendy and her colleagues, but it wasn't all plain sailing for the young stewardess.

"In the Blue Corner..."

"It happened in 1988 during the Air Traffic Controllers dispute," she remembered. "We were waiting six hours on board a *Boeing 757* at Gatwick before being cleared for take-off. Our destination was Alicante, Spain, where there would be a quick turn-around to bring a full load of passengers back home again."

It wasn't until the *757* was on its final approach to Alicante that the problems began...

"We were told that the flaps on the port wing had locked out," said Wendy. "This presented a big technical problem, and although it didn't prevent our captain making a perfect landing, it would have to be sorted out before we could take-off again."

After a brief discussion with the Spanish engineers, the captain decided, in the interests of safety, to have our own Airline engineers flown in to deal with the malfunctioning flaps. This, unfortunately, meant further delays to those passengers who had already been kept waiting for their return flight.

"They'd been stuck in that terminal building for almost twelve hours when our number one stewardess decided to send two of us to check on their welfare," said Wendy ruefully.

"As soon as we stepped into the building and the passengers caught sight of our uniforms, we were literally mobbed. It soon became obvious that, despite the captain's request, they had not been informed of the reason for the delay."

Recalling the ugly scenes that followed, the stewardess still found room for a measure of understanding at the passengers behaviour.

"They were all very hot, tired and extremely frustrated at the long delay, particularly the mums with babies to contend with. A lot of them had run out of baby food and were generally sick to death with the whole world and airlines in particular," she smiled. "There was no calming them, and I'd got separated from my friend, so it was a bit scary to say the least."

Drawing on all her training, Wendy sought desperately to calm things down and tried to explain the reason for the delay. Just as she appeared to be winning the day, a very angry young mum pushed through the throng and confronted the startled stewardess.

"She wasn't going to be pacified, that was obvious," said Wendy. "I tried sympathising with her because of the plight her baby was in, but that didn't work. I tried logic, reasoning, understanding – the lot. I couldn't have done very well because the next thing is, she's handing baby to dad and squaring up for fisticuffs. I swear the crowd opened up to form a ring but this was probably my imagination."

Wendy was still trying to talk her way out of the confrontation when the infuriated passenger launched herself forward with fists flying.

"Luckily, her husband managed to grab hold of her and held her back. I got out of there PDQ (pretty damn quick!) and dashed back to the aircraft to report the situation."

Re-united with her fellow stewardess, who had also escaped from the throng, Wendy expressed her fears about the flight home.

"We were both a bit frightened at the thought of flying with all those angry passengers," she said. "We even asked if we could swap passengers with another aircraft that was due out the same time as us, but the captain decided that would only cause further delays."

With as much tact and diplomacy as possible, the disgruntled passengers were eventually boarded. Fears of a troubled flight, however, were soon dismissed.

"They were all so shattered by the time they got on board, that most of them were fast asleep before we'd even left the ground," laughed Wendy. "We made absolutely sure they weren't disturbed until it was time for landing back at Gatwick!"

A Cure for All Ills

During the course of an uneventful European flight, one of the stewards on board a *737* flying under the flag of one of the British airlines, was experiencing the trauma of dealing with a difficult lady passenger.

The steward's patience had been stretched to near breaking point by her incessant demands and complaints throughout the flight, and his limits of endurance had almost been reached. As yet another summons from the dissatisfied passenger brought him down the cabin, he braced himself for the next confrontation.

"Steward, I've got a sore throat," she stated flatly as he stood attentively over her.

"I'm sorry to hear that, Madam," he proffered solicitously, awaiting further instructions.

"Well, I'd like something for it," she demanded as though wondering why the hapless steward needed to be told such an obvious fact.

"I'm sorry, Madam, but we have no medication on board to cater for sore throats," he explained politely.

"Nonsense!" came the indignant reply, "Now go and get me something for it immediately."

In the light of such logic the, by now, menacingly calm steward straightened up and walked with slow, measured strides to the galley. Within minutes he was striding, with great dignity, back down the aisle, a silver salver held elegantly aloft.

On reaching the unhappy passenger, he lowered the tray and, with a flourish, whipped away the covering napkin.

"It's all I could find that may help, Madam," he said with grim satisfaction as the speechless passenger gazed transfixed at the sinister looking carving knife being proffered.

"Are you trying to suggest that I cut my throat, young man," the angry passenger asked when she'd regained her composure. "If this is your idea of a joke, I find it in very poor taste and will be making a formal complaint when we land."

With a look of injured innocence the steward picked up the knife – revealing two carefully concealed aspirins. He then used the knife to chop them skillfully into a fine powder before scooping the pain killer into a glass of water.

"Madam, I'm sure I've no idea what you are talking about," replied the steward.

As he retraced his steps to the galley, however, the rest of the passengers were delighted to see a grin of mock evil appear on his youthful features.

Not one of them gave him away.

Ear's a Good Story

Flying was still comparatively new to many of the general public and air hostess, 'Willy' Willcock recalls that a great deal of emphasis was placed on the care of 'first flighters'.

One little old lady, Willy noticed, was listed on the waybill, not only as a 'first flighter', but also as being over eighty years old.

The *DC3* was taxiing-out for take-off, and Willy was passing out the barley sugar.

"Why are you giving everyone sweeties?" asked the old dear, as Willy offered the bowl.

"It helps to clear your ear passages," explained Willy. "Swallowing helps to clear your ears on take-off and landing."

"What's that dear?" shouted the old lady, above the engine noise.

"They're for your ears," said Willy, pointing towards her own.

Willy checked the remainder of the seat belts to make sure they were fastened, then she put away the barley sugar and returned to sit by her elderly 'first flighter' for take-off.

Imagine her amazement when she found the lady sitting happily with a piece of barley sugar sticking out of each ear!

(From 'Up Here and Down There' by Nan Witcomb, 1986 (Australia)).

"Down With the British!"

An American Airline, patriotic to the core, decided to mark the annual War of Independence celebrations by presenting commemorative medallions to every passenger booked on their July 4th flights. These would be handed out by the stewardesses during the flight, accompanied by a free glass of champagne to toast the occasion.

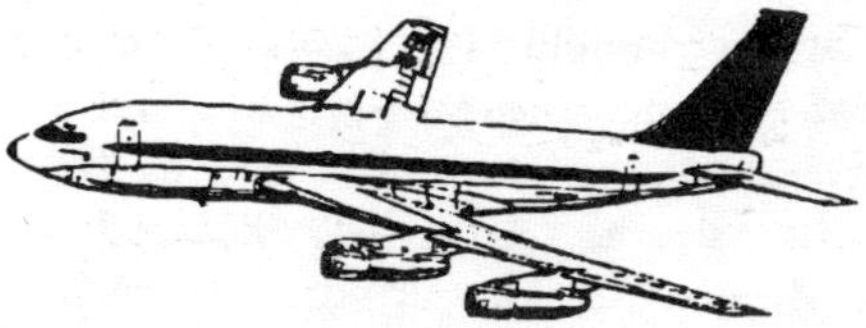

The Boeing 707

Having just informed her passengers of the forthcoming treat, a young American stewardess on one of the Airline's *707s* smiled at the enthusiastic reception her announcement had received. Rebel yells and whoops of delight filled the cabin as the aircraft flew high over the Atlantic. Amidst the uproar, a laughing voice rose above the clamour.

"What about us?—We're British."

Quickly pinpointing the little group of Britons, the stewardess addressed them over the loudspeaker system.

"That's okay by us, Sir. You're welcome to join in our celebrations but if you feel it's your duty not to fraternise with the enemy, then I'll show you the door!"

A burst of laughter greeted the stewardess's words and the American passengers turned to the beleaguered group of Britons to see what response, if any, would be given.

A short, huddled discussion took place between the outnumbered Englishmen, followed by the almost magical appearance of several souvenir American flags from their cabin bags. With shouts of, "Down with the British" and "God bless America," the cheerful turncoats vigorously waved the 'Stars and Stripes' high in the air—to the roaring approval of the Americans.

When the time came for the medallions and champagne to be brought around, the young stewardess who had crossed swords with the British group approached them with tray in hand.

"Here you are, gentlemen, with our compliments and admiration," she smiled.

As the tray was lowered, it became obvious that the medallions had been altered slightly for the British contingent. Neatly taped to the face of the coins, hand-written tags proclaimed, 'American War of Independence—Runners-up'.

Domestic Strife

A very haughty lady, flying first class on a transatlantic *Stratocruiser* flight, was giving one of the English air stewardesses a very hard time. The lady's manner and incessant demands had proved extremely trying for the stewardess who happened to be one of BOAC's more upper-crust employees.

As the aircraft began its descent into London, the luckless stewardess had been summoned yet again by the strident voice of her tormentor.

"Miss, what is the form regarding domestic servants in London these days?" she brayed arrogantly for all to hear.

"Very good indeed, Madam," replied the stewardess with deadly sweetness, "You should find no difficulty at all in securing a position!"

A Question of Taste

A South African lady passenger, en-route to her home country on one of the early flying-boat services, had been flirting outrageously with all the male crew-members during the course of the flight. Considerable embarrassment had been endured, particularly by the young steward, and it was with some trepidation that he approached the brash South African with the after-lunch refreshment...

"Coffee, Madam?" he enquired, bracing himself for the inevitable suggestive response.

"Yes please, handsome," she replied huskily, "I'll have it as I like my men – hot and strong."

"Black or white, madam?" the steward asked with devastating innocence.

Lightning Strike

From out of the heart of a violent winter's storm there came the uneven roar of a low-flying aircraft. Even the hardy Swiss, those not already indoors, paused long enough to glance skywards with apprehension. Such a night was meant for shelter and warmth, with perhaps a warming glass of schnapps to keep out the winter chill—not for putting your life at risk in the frail metal confines of an aeroplane.

The darkness was ripped aside as yet another flash of lightning illuminated the driving snow with ghostly luminesence. For a brief moment those on the ground caught sight of the aircraft, a *Vickers Vanguard*, as it descended through the storm. They marvelled at its apparent invincibility and the skill of its crew, before turning their collars up and hurrying home.

On board the *Vanguard*, a party of British schoolchildren, on their way to Saltzburg for a ski-ing holiday, were being subjected to all the terrors of flying through heavy turbulence.

Stewardess, Sally Reilly* takes up the story...

"The children were very frightened and we had our work cut-out dealing with all the sick cases," she recalled. "You could see the snow pelting down outside and all the time these huge flashes of lightning kept shooting past. The aircraft was being thrown all over the place and it was a real struggle to try and stay on our feet."

As the pilot descended in readiness for the final landing approach, battling constantly with the controls, a piercing shard of lightning lanced out of the darkness and struck the *Vanguard* half way down the starboard fuselage.

"It shot straight through the cabin," said Sally incredulously. "It came in on the starboard side and out again on the port."

'Whadd'ya mean, 'conductor'? I thought we were on a plane!'

The *Vanguard* shuddered under the impact and an acrid smell of burning filled the cabin.

"The luggage racks caught the full impact—there were long, smouldering scorch marks where the lightning had struck," she remembered. "I don't know what effect the strike had on the aircraft's performance but we overshot the runway on our first landing attempt."

The stricken airliner banked over and flew back into the teeth of the storm for a second approach.

"We were still being thrown all over the sky," said the stewardess. "The children were very good but, understandably, even more frightened than before. There was this horrible smell of scorching upholstery and smoke was curling away from the luggage racks."

Again the *Vanguard* turned on final approach and again the captain sought to bring his passengers safely to earth.

Correcting each violent movement with sure and skilful handling, the grim-faced pilot sought desperately to line his aircraft up on the snow-blanketed runway ahead – the ferocity of the storm seemingly intent on denying him the chance of overcoming this last obstacle.

"We could feel the aircraft descending and everyone was praying like mad that we'd get down safely this time," remembered Sally. "Strangely enough, I never felt that we wouldn't make it. That aircraft was a tough old bird and the crew were very experienced."

Sally's confidence proved well founded as the undercarriage wheels made contact with the runway.

With barely a bounce, they were down.

"It was a marvellous piece of flying," said the stewardess with feeling.

Pale-faced and shaken, the party of schoolchildren trooped thankfully off the battered *Vanguard*, their thoughts turning quickly to the holiday in front of them. With the resilience of the very young, the trauma of their recent experience would soon be forgotten, to be replaced with a certain pride in the shared adventure.

It would be nice to think that they took the time to glance briefly at the aeroplane and its crew and to offer, perhaps, a silent word of thanks for their deliverance from the storm.

It would be impossible to relate every adventure that befell air stewards and stewardesses during the course of their varied careers. Suffice to say that the immaculate, smiling figure that welcomes you aboard your holiday flight may well be harbouring a positive wealth of unusual experiences. Many stewardesses still ruefully recall the jokes played on them as recently graduated trainees, such as...

Standing nervously in the aircraft cabin awaiting the arrival of passengers who have already left the terminal building and, suddenly, finding themselves bundled unceremoniously into one of the overhead luggage racks – a position from which it is almost impossible to extricate oneself without assistance!

Of having to complete an emergency ditching drill in front of a full complement of passengers whilst comically encased in a fully inflated lifejacket that had mysteriously replaced the non-inflatable demonstration model...

Or even being taken-in by the captain's explanation that the reason for the aircraft's drop in flying speed had nothing at all to do with strong head winds, merely the fact that they were going 'uphill'!

For the majority of airline passengers, stewards and stewardesses will be compared with waiters and waitresses, serving in-flight meals and fetching and carrying the odd drink as required. For others, the story is different...

A terrified lady passenger, trying desperately hard to conceal her fear of flying, will forever remember the perceptiveness of the young stewardess who saw through her thin veneer of confidence.

"Just before take-off, she knelt down beside me and squeezed my hand," remembered the grateful passenger. "She just whispered, 'Don't worry, this is the safest aeroplane in the world and the captain is the best pilot I've ever flown with.' Even as we were taking-off, she kept turning around to smile at me as though to say, 'There you are – easy isn't it? I'll never forget that girl as long as I live."

For those passengers with reason to remember the calm courage of cabin staff in times of crisis and emergency, there is no comparison at all. Mercifully few though these occasions are, they require instant action and cool thinking. That cabin crews are rarely found wanting in these situations speaks highly for the selection and training methods employed by the various airlines.

British Airways, for example, will select only three out of every one hundred applicants vying for the post of air steward or stewardess. In a tough, two-day interview, they are assessed on their potential ability to provide a very high standard of customer service.

"We look for people with a proven track record for dealing with the public," explained a BA spokesman. "Anyone with a background of experience in travel agencies or building societies would be considered. We even find that ex-bar staff, with their flair for dealing with demanding customers, make excellent candidates."

The training covers a huge range of necessary skills required by cabin staff, and the trainees are tested to the limit of their ability.

Service routines; customer care; medical training; emergency procedures – all are dealt with at great length.

"They've got to be able to meet and deal with any crisis that may occur in the air," emphasised an instructor. "There's no-one to turn to when you're three miles high. Obviously, they aren't doctors but they are trained to a standard very much higher than the ordinary first-aider."

Cardiac arrests; unconsciousness; unexpected births; the use of oxygen; how to cope with invalid passengers; children; animals and any other problem they are likely to encounter is covered extensively in a programme designed to bring out the very best in the young trainees.

Emergency drills are taught in realistic cabin simulators and it's the startling realism of these exercises that stay in the minds of all who pass through the portals of BA's training school. Evacuation techniques in the event of forced landings on land and over the sea are practised until the trainee's reactions become second nature and highly disciplined.

Humour, even when training for the very worst eventuality, is never very far from the surface. Stewardess, Wendy Walker, remembers the time she spent in one of her own Airline's cabin simulators...

"We were in a 757 simulator at the time," she recalls. "It must have been all of twenty feet off the ground and there was absolute bedlam going on during this particular exercise. The training steward, who was a real character, had decided that he would be an unconscious passenger on this occasion and promptly threw himself on the floor in front of the exit."

With the smoke machine filling the cabin with murky darkness, flashing lights simulating fire and cases being thrown about the enclosed space, the girls were experiencing all the effects of a crash landing.

"We trampled all over the training steward first of all," laughed Wendy. "That went down really well, as you can imagine. For a supposed unconscious man he made a very good job of, shall we say, describing our shortcomings!"

An attempt to rectify the situation also met with disaster.

"We decided to pick him up and carry him to safety," revealed Wendy. "Unfortunately, the girl struggling with the 'talking end' lost her grip and dropped him with an awful thud!"

Crawling with exaggerated movements to the rear of the cabin, the battered steward waved away all further rescue attempts.

"He said he'd probably be a lot safer and stand a much better chance of survival if he stayed with the doomed aeroplane," grinned Wendy.

Humorous though this incident was, the stewardess was quick to point out that the training she received at the training school was second to none.

"It was very impressive," she stated. "At the end of the course we felt ready for anything."

The wings awarded to successful trainees are hard-won and much coveted. Worn with enormous pride, they symbolise a profession that is both respected and admired by millions, yet it would only be with the greatest of difficulty that you could convince any of them that they are a cut above the normal. During the course of our meeting, stewardess, Sally Reilly* expressed concern that her story ('lightning strike'), might put people off flying altogether. In company with every other steward/stewardess who helped in the compilation of this chapter, she retains a tremendous loyalty to the airline she flew with (not named at her own request) and a deep love of flying.

It was with some reluctance that she related the above incident to me, feeling that her own part in it was insignificant and that it might not be in the best interests of promoting flying as a safe form of travel.

My own belief is that passengers will find a certain amount of reassurance from the realisation that they are in the care of such professionally competent flight deck officers and cabin crew. Emergency situations occur in all walks of life and flying is no exception. It speaks well for the design and manufacture of modern airliners and the expertise and sheer professionalism of their crews that so few of these emergencies fail to respond to competent remedial action.

During the course of my research into this chapter, I also received a letter from Judy Davis ('Judy's Story') in which she expressed surprise that I should wish to highlight her side of the story. Like so many others of her calling, Judy believes that she was just an ordinary person who happened to get caught up in an extraordinary event.

I felt moved to reply that I, along with many others, would disagree with her opinion. Air stewards and stewardesses, whatever their title, are a breed apart. Courteous, competent, courageous – call them what you will.

Ordinary, they are not!

'Tea? Coffee? Our would you prefer a paper bag?'

Chapter 4

"In Case of Emergency"

The powerful thrust of four Rolls Royce *RB211* aero engines lifted British Airways *Boeing 747, City of Edinburgh* into the clear night sky over the Malaysian capital of Kuala Lumpur. The year was 1982 – the *747's* take-off was logged at 8.00pm local time – destination Perth, Australia.

For the 247 passengers and 16 crew members of BA flight 009, it was the beginning of a nightmare adventure that would bring the primeval forces of nature's deadliest emissary into direct and savage conflict with modern technology and human tenacity.

It would also dispel for ever, the myth that modern day pilots are incapable of flying by the seat of their pants!

Thirty minutes into the ill-fated journey the *747*, call sign Speedbird 9 passed over Jakarta on the west coast of Java. On the flight deck, Captain Eric Moody took a long, hard look at his weather radar screen as his co-pilot, First Officer Roger Greaves made a routine radio transmission to the local ground control.

"Jakarta control, Speedbird 9 over Halim Airport. Level 370."

Eric, finding nothing to concern himself with on the weather front, handed over to First Officer Greaves and, with a passing word to Flight Engineer Barry Townley-Freeman, made his way aft to the lower deck washroom.

Within minutes, he was recalled to the flight deck by the urgent summons of his number one stewardess, Fiona Wright.

The scene that greeted him on his return to the cockpit was one of eerie wonder. The aircraft appeared to be under intense bombardment from a barrage of luminous white sparks that were hurtling out of the darkness to explode in silent splendour against the front windscreen. The amazing pyrotechnic display provided a breathtaking performance for the three airmen, who believed at the time that they were witnessing an exceptionally strong and concentrated form of St Elmo's Fire.

They nonetheless took the precaution of strapping themselves in and ensured that the passengers did likewise.

Glancing out of the side windows, both pilots were startled to see the mighty Rolls Royce engines glowing vividly as though illuminated from within and, on facing forward again, they encountered yet another phenomenon. The original St Elmo's Fire effect had been replaced by streams of straight line luminosity that looked remarkably like tracer bullets flying directly at them.

With barely time to comprehend the rapidly changing sequence of events, Eric heard his First Officer call out sharply.

"Engine failure number 4!"

Instinct and training came to the fore as the emergency compounded itself, and all three crew members reacted instantly. Roger and Barry swiftly carried out the engine fire drill on Eric's instructions until...

"Engine failure number 2!"

"Three's gone, Eric."

"They've all gone!"

The unthinkable had happened. Four of the most reliable engines in the world had failed, and 300 tons of *Jumbo Jet* began to nose down towards the Indian Ocean, seven miles below.

"Jakarta, Jakarta, Mayday, Mayday, Speedbird 9. We've lost all four engines. We're leaving 370."

First Officer Roger Greaves' transmission was not immediately understood by the Jakarta ground controller and his reply, when it came, did more to raise the co-pilot's blood pressure than the predicament he found himself in.

"Speedbird 9, have you got a problem?"

With some difficulty, the plight of BA flight 009 was finally conveyed to the Jakarta tower via another aircraft in the vicinity.

In the passenger compartments, meanwhile, emotions were running high as the cabin crew sought desperately to calm their frightened passengers. Many believed the engines were on fire and that a crash landing in the sea was inevitable. Others thought the thickening smoke haze would suffocate them first.

First Officer Greaves and Flight Engineer Townley-Freeman tried again and again to re-ignite the silent engines—to no avail. The *747* was now descending at over 2000ft a minute!

The strident sound of the cabin pressure warning horn cut through the confined space of the flight deck, warning of yet another danger. Oxygen masks would now have to be fitted quickly to avoid the effects of Anoxia, a dangerously disabling affliction that results in unconsciousness.

Eric and Barry swiftly donned their masks but fate had not yet finished with flight 009.

First Officer Roger Greaves' mask fell to pieces in his hands!

Eric Moody was left with two unenviable options. Either he could maintain his present rate of descent and buy a little extra time or he could ensure his First Officer's safety by bringing the *747* rapidly down to a lower level where normal breathing would be possible.

Without hesitation, Eric exerted a steady forward pressure on the control column and the *747's* nose angled sharply downwards. Speedbird 9, with all its engines silent, began to drop out of the sky in an emergency dive.

At 20,000ft, Roger managed to piece together his oxygen mask and Eric was able, at last, to bring the *747* out of its dive. At this point, he felt that the passengers should be informed of the situation and switched on the cabin intercom.

"Good evening ladies and gentlemen, this is your captain speaking. We have a small problem. All our engines have stopped. We are all doing our damndest to get them going again. I trust you are not in too much distress."

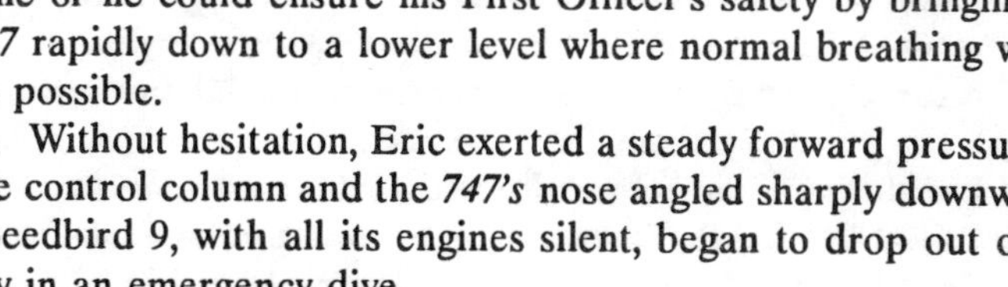

'If they've lost the engines, where did they put them last?'

British Airways Captain, Eric Moody would be a great disappointment to the Royal Academy of Dramatic Arts!

His words had the desired effect on at least one of his passengers however, who was heard to remark:

"Thank God for that – I thought we were in big trouble for a moment!"

Speedbird 9 continued to lose height, dropping through 13,500ft in its inexorable descent towards the ghostly, shimmering sea far below. Eric began to think ahead, towards the possibility of a ditched landing in the vastness of the Indian Ocean, and did not relish the prospect.

With a sudden, surging roar, number four engine re-ignited!

Ninety seconds later, at a height of 12,000ft, the other three burst into joyous life and a buoyant Roger Greaves lost no time in radioing the good news.

"Speedbird 9, we're back in business. All four engines running. Level 12,000."

The three men shared a few moments of jubilation as Eric brought the control column back to regain the precious height they'd lost during their enforced descent. It wasn't to last...

At 15,000ft they flew head on into a resumption of the St Elmo's Fire that had preceded their earlier problems and, almost immediately, the number two engine surged frighteningly. The aircraft began to vibrate alarmingly and Eric, very reluctantly, shut the offending engine down completely. At this point he concluded that the cause of their predicament lay at altitude and quickly sought safety below 15,000ft.

Nursing the three damaged engines carefully, Eric turned the crippled *747* on a heading back towards Jakarta's Halim Airport. He sought vainly to locate the runway lights, realising eventually that a new peril had presented itself.

Speedbird 9 was blind!

The front windscreen had apparently been blasted by some unknown force that had left it so badly scored and stained that forward vision for the two pilots was almost non-existent.

The fate of 260 souls now lay in the hands of three British airmen and a battle-scarred American *Jumbo Jet*. The odds, it seemed, were heavily stacked on the side of the grim reaper!

The *Boeing 747*, however, was a very tough bird indeed and the three airmen, in the words of one Australian journalist, were best described as, "Obstinate bastards with an irreverent disregard for the inevitable."

The combination was formidable.

First Officer Greaves switched on the *747's* landing lights in a desperate attempt to provide some form of illumination for the blind landing ahead of them.

Nothing!

The landing-light covers had sustained the same damage as the windscreen and were practically useless.

Eric finally managed to locate a tiny strip of clear windscreen, about three inches wide, on the outer edge of the front cockpit window—just enough for him to make out the left hand edge of the main runway.

But in this cramped position he could not see the instrument readings that were so vital for a safe touchdown.

As the final minutes ticked agonizingly by, the flight deck crew of BA flight 009 became as one in their concerted effort to bring the mighty airliner safely back to earth.

First Officer Roger Greaves and Flight Engineer Barry Townley-Freeman called out repeated height and speed checks as Captain Eric Moody, flying by instinct and the 'seat of his pants' gently eased the stricken airliner towards the unseen ground beneath them.

Speedbird 9 swooped over the runway threshold at 150 knots, sinking ever lower towards the unyielding concrete below.

In a remarkable display of precision flying, Captain Eric Moody 'flared' (levelled off) the shuddering *747* and settled her feather-light on the welcoming runway of Halim Airport.

Speedbird 9, battered but unbowed, had returned to earth.

Aftermath

Two days later, the cause of the emergency was revealed. Mount Galunggung, an active volcano lying menacingly off the Java coast, had erupted with devastating fury on the evening of 24th June. Such was the force of the eruption that a huge, all-enveloping, cloud of volcanic debris was sent hurtling over eight miles into the air – straight into the path of flight 009.

Like some primeval monster of old, it had engulfed the *747* and sought to choke the life out of it.

Speedbird 9, shredding to pieces the adage that a good big 'un will always beat a good little 'un, had emerged from the maelstrom triumphantly victorious.

Quotable Quotes

Humour will rise to the surface on almost any occasion and the Jakarta emergency was no exception. During the emotional scenes that followed the safe landing of flight 009, much praise was directed at the flight deck crew, yet it was to be the back-handed compliment of a distraught Australian girl as she was led sobbing from the aircraft that would stick in everyone's minds for its heartfelt simplicity.

"I'll never rubbish the poms again!" she vowed.

Eric Moody, much to his surprise, was lauded as a hero by the world's press and suffered endless questioning with great fortitude. Some of the questions directed at him invited swatting at birth, and one in particular led to a quote that really ought to guarantee immortality for the man who, in his own words, "Went gliding in a *747*."

"What was it like to land in the dark with no forward vision?" he was asked.

Eric, a Hampshire man to the core and a very eloquent speaker to boot, thought carefully before imparting his eagerly awaited pearls of wisdom.

"It was," he replied with great relish, "like negotiating one's way up a badger's arse!"

'I like badgers, I've always liked badgers...'

A Breath of Fresh Air

Sunday June 10th 1990 was already being heralded as a pre-dawn of destiny for England as Captain Tim Lancaster strode out to the parking bay at Birmingham Airport where British Airways *BAC1-11, County of South Glamorgan* sat in gleaming splendour awaiting his arrival.

Jack Charlton's Republic of Ireland football team were threatening to walk all over Bobby Robson's England squad in the opening round of the World Cup the following night, and the nation looked forward with expectation to the outcome of the clash.

At forty-one, Tim was of a like age to the England goalkeeper, Peter Shilton, but it was to be the safe hands of his crew, not the goalkeeper's, that would dominate the headlines the following day...

On the flight deck, Captain Lancaster finalised his pre-flight cockpit checks alongside his co-pilot, First Officer Alistair Atchison. In the cabin, Purser, John Heward, noted with satisfaction that the two air stewards, Nigel Ogden and Simon Rogers, along with stewardess, Susan Prince, had settled their eighty one passengers in readiness for take-off – destination Malaga.

The *BAC1-11* rolled smoothly down the runway and lifted off into the morning sunlight.

Flight 5390 was airborne and on its way to the Mediterranean.

The time had just turned 8.30am and flight 5390 was climbing over Oxfordshire through 17,300ft. Steward, Nigel Ogden, with his colleagues busy serving refreshments to the passengers, was in the forward galley, closest to the flight deck.

Everything was as it should be – peaceful and relaxed.

The tranquillity was shattered in a split second when the main windscreen in front of Tim Lancaster blew out with explosive violence!

The force of the decompression literally tore him from his seat belt and hurled him towards the 3ft opening. The flight-deck door, slamming open in the rush of air, had been ripped off its hinges, allowing Steward Ogden in the forward galley to see immediately the plight of his skipper.

Reacting instantly, he raced into the cockpit and threw himself at the fast disappearing legs of the hapless pilot. In the desperate struggle that followed, Nigel Ogden's right arm was badly gashed, weakening further his already precarious hold on Tim's legs.

'Was it something I said?'

The forward speed of the *BAC1-11*, in excess of 500mph, created a slipstream that battered the pilot's body against the side of the aircraft and threatened to tear it from the grasp of the injured and exhausted steward. The outside temperature at 17,300ft was a freezing minus 20-degrees centigrade, and it was the intense cold that Tim remembered just before losing consciousness.

The pilot's shirt had been ripped from his back by the force of the decompression, leaving him pinned, half-naked and helpless against the side of the *County of South Glamorgan.*

First Officer Alistair Atchison, fully occupied with the task of controlling the aircraft, was powerless to help in the life or death struggle and, indeed, had been lucky not to have suffered the same fate as his captain. Had he not been wearing full safety harness, and had steward Ogden not prevented Tim Lancaster from being sucked completely out of the gaping hole, he would almost certainly have been swept to his death.

The chances of survival for the other four crew members and eighty-one passengers would then have been practically non-existent!

Just as Nigel Ogden began to feel his strength slipping away, he became aware of steward, Simon Rogers alongside him in the cockpit. With great presence of mind, Simon climbed into the jump-seat, located behind the captain's seat and strapped himself in. Safely anchored, he then wrapped his arms tightly around Tim Lancaster, relieving Nigel of his terrible burden.

Alistair Atchison, at the first sign of trouble, had immediately put the aircraft into a steep spiral dive to bring them down into breathable air-space. His mayday emergency call had already been acknowledged by ground control.

Back in the passenger cabin, Purser John Heward and stewardess, Susan Prince had their work cut out trying to calm the passengers and prepare them for an emergency landing. All of them had heard the explosion as the windscreen blew out, and those at the front of the aircraft could clearly see the drama being enacted in the cockpit – a sight that some could not bear to look at.

Flying a *BAC1-11* single-handed is considered a very demanding job at the best of times, but First Officer Atchison was not enjoying the best of times! Not only did he have a damaged aircraft to handle, he had the distraction of the frantic struggle still taking place right next to him, and the grim thought that a heavy landing could seriously injure his skipper or, even worse, dislodge him.

The slight jolt as the landing gear dropped into place warned the passengers that they were now on the final approach to an emergency touchdown. All assumed the brace position on the instructions of the cabin staff.

Flight 5390, with its captain hanging unconscious from the remains of the front windscreen, was returning, prematurely, to earth.

Battling with the controls, First Officer Alistair Atchison eased the big jet gingerly towards the runway's outer markers. Southampton Airport was only just big enough to accommodate the *BAC1-11* and he would need every inch of the short runway to bring it safely to a halt.

Holding his breath, Alistair gently drew back on the control column and flight 5390 sank out of the sky for a perfect touchdown. Not a tremor could be felt as he applied the brakes for one of the smoothest landings of his career.

Captain Tim Lancaster was still draped over the nose section of the aeroplane. Nobody, at that stage, knew whether he was alive or dead.

Gently, he was lowered to the ground and rushed to Southampton General Hospital where his condition, amazingly, was found to be "not serious." Several minor fractures and frostbite from exposure to the freezing air were his only legacies from one of the most incredible and dangerous aerial incidents ever recorded.

England and Ireland drew their match in Calgiari the following evening. Tim Lancaster's gallant crew, at the other end of the scale and with a great deal more at stake than the World Cup, had achieved far more with their undisputed victory in one of the biggest and loneliest arenas known to man – the sky!

Endpiece:

Accident investigators discovered that eighty-four of the ninety bolts used to fit the *BAC1-11's* window were too short for the purpose and, consequently, were unable to withstand the pressure as flight 5390 gained height over Oxfordshire. The window, still intact, crashed to the ground on a deserted farm track.

They Always come in Threes.

One month prior to Tim Lancaster's 'extra-vehicular sojourn' on flight 5390 an almost carbon copy incident occurred on board a *Fairchild* airliner over Seattle in the United States.

The aircraft was at 14,000ft when one of the starboard cabin windows suddenly blew out. National Guard Major, Gayle Sears was dragged from his seat restraint by the decompression and the top half of his body was sucked clean through the cavity into the driving rain outside. The prompt action of two of his fellow passengers saved him from certain death and he was quickly hauled back inside the cabin.

The *Fairchild* made a successful landing, leaving a shocked and very relieved Gayle Sears declaring:

"I came within an inch of meeting the prophet – it was that close!"

The third incident, incredibly, took place on the ground. A stewardess on board a Canadian Airlines jet was saved from a similar fate by one of her colleagues who held on to her as the airliner made an emergency stop on the runway.

Trips outside an aircraft in flight are, fortunately, very rare, but they are not unique to modern jetliners. Neither were they all involuntary...

In 1924, a lumbering *Farman Goliath* bi-plane took off from Croydon Aerodrome with eight passengers on board bound for Paris. The huge machine, powered by two *Salmson* radial engines affixed to the lower wing, had a cruising speed of 75mph only and closely resembled a wooden crate with wings.

On this occasion, the aircraft's mechanic sat alongside the pilot in the tiny open cockpit situated just forward of the massive wings. The problem arose shortly after take off.

The throttle control had broken, leaving the pilot with two options. Either he could undertake a forced landing without the vital mechanism or an attempt could be made to hand operate the throttle. His mechanic had no hesitation in recommending the second course of action, even though it meant he would have to crawl out on to the starboard wing to carry out the operation!

Complete with full leather flying clothing, tightly buckled helmet and goggles protecting his eyes from the slipstream, the intrepid mechanic clambered from the cockpit and edged his way precariously towards the vibrating wing – in full view of the terrified passengers.

Positioning himself alongside the roaring engine he proceeded to manually operate the throttle and continued to do so for the best part of an hour until the pilot put them down safely at Lympne airfield.

The shaken passengers were disembarked and arrangements made for them to fly on to Paris in another aircraft.

'Carry on with your gin & tonics, don't worry about me.'

All except one.

He had watched the whole episode, mesmerized with fear, from one of the cabin windows and had elected to carry on by boat and train!

Tim Lancaster's unscheduled stopover in Southampton became one more statistic to log in a series of aeroplane related incidents over Hampshire. In May of the same year a block of ice plummetted from a high flying airliner and narrowly missed a school at North Baddesley on the western outskirts of Southampton. A similar incident occurred three weeks later, this time in the New Forest. Incredibly, another drama was to unfold in the skies over Hampshire before the year was out...

On the 20th August a South African *747 Jumbo Jet*, piloted by Captain Gavin Fouche, took off from Heathrow at 6.55pm, destination Johannesburg.

The Jumbo had a V.I.P on board – Archbishop Desmond Tutu.

The aircraft had barely left the runway when it flew straight into a flock of geese – with disastrous results. The *747* shuddered under the impact and actually struck the runway as Captain Fouche fought to lift it into the air.

At first, everybody feared the worse, believing that the geese had been sucked into the engines but, luckily, this wasn't the case. They had, however, smashed into a fibreglass panel on the undersurface of one of the wings and Captain Fouche was immediately diverted out over Basingstoke, Winchester and Southampton with instructions to burn off fuel prior to returning to Heathrow for an emergency landing.

On the ground, Southampton man, Dave Tidworthy watched the airliner as it passed overhead.

"There were two long streamers of fuel pouring out of the wingtips," he recalled. "I trained my binoculars on it and suddenly saw something detach from the plane. I don't know what it was but I could see it glinting in the sunlight as it spiralled down. It looked like a curved piece of metal."

Captain Fouche jettisoned fuel as far out to sea as he could safely fly until the *747* had reached a safe landing weight and then turned back towards Heathrow. The question remained as to how much damage the bird strike had actually caused and whether or not it had affected the landing gear.

The *Boeing 747* proved a lot tougher than the geese though and Captain Fouche brought the stricken airliner down for a textbook landing at Heathrow.

Archbishop Tutu was quick to praise the skill of the crew and eventually returned to Johannesburg none the worse for his frightening experience.

Emergencies involving airliners are, for the number of aircraft in operational use and the amount of time they spend in the air, mercifully few. Unfortunately, incidents do occur at times to endanger some of these aircraft – incidents that are beyond the control of even the most experienced pilots. Some of them can even raise a smile.

Afterwards!

"Fangs for the Memories."

A *Lockheed Constellation* approaching Heathrow at the witching hour of midnight suddenly veered off and began circling the airport. A frantic call to the control tower indicated that the crew were experiencing problems lowering the undercarriage. Asked to confirm the problem, the captain replied in quiet desperation:

"We have a very big, extremely poisonous snake loose in the cockpit. It's wrapped around the undercarriage lever and we can't get at it to lower the gear."

The *Constellation* continued to circle for the next three hours as the sweating pilots sought desperately for a solution. Cabin staff plied the passengers with free drinks, explaining only that the delay was due to technical problems.

With fuel running dangerously low, the captain decided that an attempt, however hazardous, would have to be made to reach the undercarriage lever. The snake, by now, appeared to be asleep but this was no consolation to the two pilots. One wrong move, they felt, could unleash a venomous attack that would endanger the lives of everyone on board.

Very gently, a trembling hand reached out towards the lever and its coiled guardian. The snake's muscular body writhed lazily as it was disturbed, but it made no move to strike.

The landing gear dropped comfortingly into position.

The *Constellation* landed softly on the runway in one of the smoothest landings ever witnessed at Heathrow.

Sheer terror, it seems, makes an excellent co-pilot!

The vet who boarded the aircraft identified the reptile as a harmless King Snake, one of the most docile creatures in the world.

However, he felt it prudent not to mention this at the time!

Lucky "Connie"

In the days of the 'short strip' at Hong Kong Airport, long before the big new runway was built, a *749 Constellation* (or *'Connie'* as they were affectionately known) of BOAC had just settled on to its final landing approach. On this particular runway it was not possible to abort a landing in the final stages, as the towering hill at the far end was too near and too large to avoid. In other words, the captain was committed to a landing no matter what hazard presented itself at the last minute.

As he 'flared' for, touchdown a Chinese woman ran straight into the path of the aircraft and stood, it seemed, waiting for certain death.

'Rest assured, your luck's about to run out completely.'

"I just managed to lift my starboard wing over her and landed rather shakily a bit further down the runway," recalled the astonished captain.

"I was bloody furious and played hell with the controller," he grinned, "He was a little frayed around the edges as well, and asked me to call at the control tower before going on to our hotel."

The unfortunate Chinese woman had been unceremoniously bundled into one of the airport trucks and brought before the irate controller.

"There was a lot of shouting in Chinese going on when I arrived at the tower," related the pilot. "From what I could gather, the lady had suffered a year of considerable bad luck and, as this was Chinese New Year, she was determined to improve her lot for the coming year."

Superstition had it that if you could get your shadow run-over on New Year's Eve, it would exorcize the bad luck and ensure good fortune for the year ahead.

"Her reasoning, that a *'Connie'* cast a bloody sight bigger shadow than anything else and therefore would bring extra luck, couldn't be faulted," continued the pilot, "But if I hadn't managed to lift that wing up all the luck in the world wouldn't have helped her!"

Amidst a great deal of gesticulating and remonstration, the controller finally asked the bemused captain if he wanted to prosecute the tearful woman.

"I told him that if anyone needed prosecuting, it was the airport authorities for allowing anyone unauthorised to get on to the runway in the first place," he said.

"That went down really well. I'm not sure what he screamed at me as I left because it was in Chinese, but I feel it wasn't, 'Happy New Year'!"

It wasn't Chinese New Year when Captain Ming Yuan Ho took off from Taiwan in a China Airlines *747* but he was about to use up all his luck anyway, in one stomach-wrenching moment of high drama over the Pacific Ocean.

At 40,000ft, on course for Los Angeles, the number four engine suffered a malfunction. Despite repeated attempts at reignition the flagging engine eventually cut-out altogether and the *747* began to roll to starboard.

Captain Ming disengaged the auto-pilot in readiness for a manual descent – with shocking and devastating results.

The *747* flipped on to its back and plummeted out of the sky at almost three miles a minute!

Taken completely by surprise, the pilot was horrified to feel the aircraft starting to spin out of control and fought desperately to bring it back on to an even keel.

The aircraft, at this stage, was being subjected to forces of gravity way in excess of its design limit and these same forces were pinning Captain Ming to his seat, severely restricting his mobility.

The scene in the passenger cabin was one of total chaos. Those not strapped into their seats were hurled around like rag dolls, along with every other loose object in sight. Cabin staff were powerless to help, their predicament being as perilous as their passengers.

Captain Ming struggled frantically to regain control of the aircraft, his movements hampered by the fierce 'G' forces. He was fighting a losing battle but refused to accept the inevitable – a trait common among airline pilots. He needed something more than skill to help him now and it came in a strangely backhanded way.

The undercarriage mechanism failed, sending the huge wheels shuddering down to lock into place!

Luck takes many strange forms but, for Captain Ming, this didn't appear to be one of them. In fact, it seemed as though everything that could go wrong on a *Jumbo* was being demonstrated to him with vindictive malice.

He was more than happy to be proven wrong.

The massive undercarriage dropping into position had acted like a giant air-brake, slowing down the rate of descent and easing the *747* out of its terrifying spin.

Captain Ming seized his opportunity and, with a superhuman effort and extraordinary flying skill, regained control of his aerobatically minded *747*. He set course for San Francisco.

One hour later, to thunderous applause from his passengers (none of whom suffered serious injury), Captain Ming Yuan Ho landed flight 006 safely and smoothly on the runway at San Francisco Airport.

The captain of a *DC8*, making the same approach to San Francisco some years earlier had not been so lucky, despite having the advantage of a perfectly sound aircraft...

Visibility, at the time of this amazing incident, was practically non-existent. The pilot of the *DC8*, his eyes aching with the strain of peering into the gloom, guided his aircraft down through the clouds in readiness for the final landing approach.

Nothing, at this stage, gave any indication of the drama that was about to unfold...

The landing gear came down with a reassuring 'thud', signalling to the weary passengers that their journey was almost at an end. Many stared out of the cabin windows, eager for a first glimpse of the friendly lights of San Francisco.

The *DC8* dropped steadily lower until the pilot finally drew back on the control column and allowed the aircraft to sink gently out of the air for a perfect touch-down – on the calm waters of San Francisco Bay!

The approach and landing had been so precise and controlled that the aircraft had ditched with scarcely a splash.

Shocked, but unhurt, crew and passengers quickly made for the emergency exits and clambered out on to the wings to await rescue.

Before the rescue operation could be set-up, however, the tide went out, leaving the *DC8* stranded high and dry on the mud-flats.

The marooned passengers then simply stepped off the wings and walked to safety!

Emergencies can take many forms—some extremely serious, others relatively minor. Passengers can often walk away from an aircraft totally unaware that they've even been involved in a crisis. Others have been known to sleep through a mid-air emergency, blissfully ignorant of the terror around them.

Flight crew can retire at the end of a long career without ever having experienced an emergency, other than in a simulator. Millions of passengers fly year in, year out without so much as a bumpy landing to mar their journey, yet the fear still persists in the minds of thousands that a crash is not only likely during the course of their flight, but inevitable.

The events related in this chapter are not intended to strengthen this belief, more are they intended to portray the fact that survival in an emergency is not only possible but highly probable.

Chapter 5

Passengers Are People Too

Without them, not one airline would survive, yet many a harassed employee has been heard to curse the very day they were all born.

They come in all shapes and sizes, are varied in colour and sex, and range in age from one to one hundred.

They can be charming, cheerful and a pleasure to deal with on the one hand and bloody-minded, demanding and a source of constant heartache on the other.

Airlines can no longer get away with dressing them in leather coats, helmets and goggles before sending them aloft with a packet of cheese sandwiches as an in-flight meal, and it would be a very unwise managing director who sought to cut costs at the expense of his paying customers.

Sometimes, sadly, they are not always treated with the reverence they feel they deserve – even though they may be heroes and celebrities in their own right.

Own Goal

The 1990 World Cup in Italy had seen several teams knocked out in the early stages, and Scotland numbered amongst them. They had played well against first class opposition and, though disappointed at the prospect of an early flight home, were certainly not returning with heads held low. An early chance to show they had not lost their sense of humour came as they approached the aircraft waiting to fly them out of Italy.

Tim Lancaster's miraculous escape after being sucked out of his *BAC1-11* (see chapter 4) was still very much in the news at the time, and the quick thinking actions of the stewards who dived to hold on to his legs was still a topic of conversation among airline crews. It was with this incident in mind that the captain of the aircraft, with tongue firmly in cheek, asked for a message to be passed to the team before they boarded. An airline representative duly addressed the players as they arrived at the foot of the passenger steps ready for boarding.

"I'm sorry, gentlemen but I'm afraid the captain is refusing to allow Jim Leighton on board."

"Why?" queried the puzzled player, wondering what he could have done to offend the pilot.

"He's worried that if the cockpit window blows out, he may have to rely on you to save him and hold on to his legs," came the reply.

Jim Leighton was the Scottish goalkeeper!

Sportsmen and women are not always ideal passengers, according to one stewardess, and even the bravest of them can harbour a fear of flying.

Some passengers are nervous of flying...

"I remember one flight," she reveals, "Muhammed Ali was on board and he was not at all happy about being up there. He admitted it was one of the few things in life that frightened him. Strangely enough," she continued, "he went up even more in my estimation after that. He was flying to keep a promise to be at a special charity function."

Others need a little 'medicinal' help to overcome their phobia... "Unfortunately," the stewardess said, "very few of them are aware that one drink at altitude can be twice as strong as two on the ground."

As one burly rugby international found to his cost...

"He was a great big feller," laughed the stewardess, "but he was absolutely terrified of flying. What I didn't know was that his mates had already given him a few glasses of 'Dutch courage' before they boarded. He seemed calm enough before take off, but then again, anybody with half a bottle of scotch inside them would be."

The calming influence of the Highland linctus had apparently evaporated on take-off.

"His mate had a quiet word with me, explaining the problem," recalled the stewardess. "He asked me to keep the whiskys coming as this would keep him calm and, hopefully, send him off to sleep. I didn't relish the thought of this lad getting too drunk, so I told them I would only serve him drinks within reason. They accepted this with surprising good will, and I went off to get the first order."

By the time the aircraft touched down at its destination, the player was fast asleep and definitely 'feeling no pain'.

"I dread to think what effect those drinks had on him at that height," grinned the stewardess, "especially as half the team had been ordering scotch and then pouring it down him as soon as my back was turned."

'He says it's for medicinal purposes.'

Although it's easy to laugh at stories such as this, it should always be remembered that, for thousands of unhappy passengers, a fear of flying is no joke at all.

This dreadful phobia can bring untold misery to its victims and, until fairly recently, there wasn't a lot you could do about it other than to grit your teeth, get drunk, or stay on the ground. Happily, there are now caring organisations to turn to for those who desperately want to find a cure. One such organisation is Relaxair, a London-based firm specialising in the field of flying phobias.

"Our philosophy is to transfer the fear of flying into an interest in flying," is how Clive Simpson, Managing Director of Relaxair, views their role.

"We've achieved a very high success rate over the years," claims Clive, "which is very gratifying for all concerned. Quite a few of our classes are taken by pilots who are excellent at knocking some of the old myths on the head."

Two of Relaxair's satisfied customers stand out in Clive's memory.

"One lady who came to us for help hadn't flown for over forty years," he recalled. "Her last flight, believe it or not, was in a Lancaster of 617 Squadron, the famous *Dambusters*. She'd been an instrument mechanic with them at the time of the raid, and after the war, had been taken on a flight over the dams as a reward for her service."

The flight out had been uneventful but the aircraft ran into rough weather on the way home.

"She had a very bad time of it on the return journey by all accounts," said Clive. "She told us she'd been absolutely terrified and couldn't bear the thought of ever going up in an aeroplane again. Happily, she took our course and is now back in the air at every available opportunity."

The second case involved another lady, who had been badgered unmercifully by her husband for over sixteen years.

"He wanted to go abroad on holiday," said Clive, "but her flying phobia made this impossible. She finally plucked up the courage to come and see us, and pretty soon felt confident enough to fly abroad with her husband."

The outward journey proved no problem whatsoever and all seemed set for a trouble free homeward leg. It was not to be...

"The aircraft hit a fair amount of turbulence on the way back," explained Clive. "Our girl wasn't affected by it – in fact, she loved every minute, but her husband went to pieces. He had a real panic attack, and it took quite a while to calm him down."

Mercifully, there is no record of his wife's comments, either in public or behind closed doors.

Thanks to organisations such as Relaxair, thousands of men and women are now enjoying the pleasures and freedom of flying without fear. They are able to take long awaited holidays abroad or, in many cases, visit loved ones living in foreign climes.

"It's a phobia that can be overcome in many cases," stresses Clive. "We're here if people want us, and most airlines will be able to provide the phone number of their nearest organisation if required."

Even those with a fervent desire to fly sometimes need assistance to get their bums in the air, and Clive's firm were on hand to help a London busman realise a long held ambition.

"Cilla Black had collared him for her 'Surprise, Surprise' television programme following a tip-off about his desire to be an airline pilot," revealed Clive. "They took him down to Northolt where this incredible bus, mocked up like an aeroplane, sat waiting on the runway for him. He had a wail of a time driving it up and down, but never actually got his feet off the ground, so we decided an invitation to fly on one of our scheduled Amsterdam flights was in order."

On his arrival at the airport, the delighted bus driver, immaculately turned out in his full London Transport uniform at Relaxair's request, discovered that he was to fly in the aircraft's 'jump' seat, located on the flight deck behind the two pilots.

"He looked splendid in his uniform," recalled Clive. "The rest of the passengers knew nothing about the treat we'd laid on for him, and we felt it only fitting that he should make a grand entrance."

The beaming bus driver was taken aboard via the rear passenger steps, allowing him to pass right through the cabin on his way to the cockpit.

"He caused quite a stir, as you can imagine," laughed Clive. "The sight of a London bus driver breezing into the cockpit just before take-off isn't something you see every day. As it turned out, everyone had a splendid flight, and we were more than pleased to have helped this very pleasant man fulfil at least part of his dream."

For every bus driver that dreams of being a pilot, there must be a conductor who harbours similar ambitions. In the heart of Scotland resides one such man who has spent almost as much time in pursuit of his dreams as he spent working for the Scottish Motor Traction Company and Eastern Scottish bus companies. He has, in the process, become known throughout his local community and, indeed, throughout the world of passenger aviation as...

'Globe' Trotter
The Flying Bus Conductor

John Trotter's first flight as an airline passenger took place on the 18th July 1945 when he paid two pounds, nine shillings for a seat on board a *Dragon Rapide* of Scottish Airways.

"I saved long and hard to pay for that ticket," he remembered. "When it was handed over to me I felt as though I'd been given the world."

From that day onwards, John deposited a small sum of money in the bank every week to pay for the many flights that were to follow, and gradually he became a familiar figure among airline crews. Captains would gladly sign his log book recording the flight, and stewardesses would pose for pictures with him in front of their aircraft – pictures that would appear in newspapers all over the world.

'Tickets please, gentlemen.'

"I loved every minute of it," said John. "When the chance came to book a seat on the inaugural flight of the British Airways *Concorde* from London to America, I couldn't wait to get my name down."

The booking was arranged on the 26th June 1964. The flight took place on the 24th May 1976.

"I could only afford the fare for the outward trip," recalled John ruefully, "I had to fly back subsonic. It was a fantastic experience though, and British Airways made a very kind gesture before the return journey."

John had gone out to Dulles Airport, Washington to watch both the Air France and BA *Concordes* take-off for the return flight. It was a very big occasion and a great many dignitaries were on hand to see the supersonic aircraft take-off.

"I was just standing nearby, looking on, when one of the British Airways executives spotted me and came over," he explained. "He shook my hand and told me with genuine regret that they'd done everything possible to get me home on *Concorde* but hadn't a single seat available. I had no idea they were even trying to find me a seat, and their efforts were much appreciated, believe me."

Not content to be a mere passive passenger, 'Globe' Trotter entered as a competitor in the Daily Mail Trans-Atlantic Air Race from the top of the GPO Tower in London to the top of the Empire State Building in New York.

"I rode pillion on a brand new 650cc Triumph motorbike from the GPO Tower to Heathrow," laughed John. "It was the most dangerous part of the whole race."

Flying with Aer Lingus, he touched down at New York and was whisked to the Empire State Building in a high-speed car laid on by Pan American.

"I made it in an official time of 8 hours 47 minutes 21.01 seconds," stated the proud competitor.

John's globetrotting was not without its share of dramatic incident either, as he recalls...

"It happened in the year that Swissair had one of their *DC-8s* blown up by terrorists," he related. "The passengers had been released but the *DC-8*, along with three other jets that had been hijacked to the desert were completely destroyed. Shortly after this event, I flew into Zurich Airport and hadn't even got to the bottom of the steps before I was confronted by a Swiss soldier pointing a machine gun at me."

The same treatment greeted John and his fellow passengers at the entrance to the terminal building, and they were alarmed to see soldiers manning heavy machine guns at all four corners of the airfield.

'Honest, it'll go 'Cuckoo' in a minute or two!'

"Whenever I visited my Swiss friends, I always bought a souvenir clock home with me and this time was no different," he continued. "Unfortunately, the girl in the shop wound it up before wrapping it and you can just imagine what happened at the airport – they thought it was a bomb."

The scene could have been straight out of one of the many comedy sketches woven around this type of incident but, for John, an additional piece of luggage lent a sinister twist to the tale.

"My friend had innocently given me a large, full colour map of Zurich Airport, complete in every detail, as a small farewell gift," he grinned. "On the back of the map was an advert, in German, for a Swiss bank. There must have been a dozen guns covering me as I was led into a cubicle for the most thorough and humiliating search I've ever had to endure."

John's ordeal ended when his passport was discovered at the bottom of his flight bag.

"They seemed surprised that I held a British passport," said the indignant Scotsman. "They had the bloody cheek to tell me that they'd mistaken me for an Arab because of my accent!"

John 'Globe' Trotter is now in his seventies, but still receives invites from airlines to fly with them on auspicious occasions. Even KLM, the Royal Dutch Airline, welcomed him as an honoured guest on board their inaugural *DC-10* flight from Amsterdam to Chicago, an indication of the high regard in which he is held everywhere.

The flying bus conductor; airline passenger extraordinary, has earned himself a deserved place in the chronicles of passenger aviation.

John Trotter has always considered himself a lucky passenger. Others have reason to believe they are related to Jonah...

Third Time Lucky?

Enid Ware's story began in 1954, when the troopship *Empire Windrush* caught fire under her thirty miles out from Algiers!

"I was returning home from Hong Kong with my husband at the time," she recalled. "We all thought we were going to sink, but luckily we were picked up by an aircraft carrier and taken on to Gibraltar. I began to think our luck had changed when they told us we were to be flown home, which was a big mistake."

Enid's visions of a luxurious civilian airliner transporting them to England on a wave of smoked salmon and cream cakes blurred and disintegrated as a battered RAF. trooping aircraft hove into view.

"I can't remember what it was exactly," she said, "but it was about the most basic and spartan aeroplane I've ever come across. We staggered into the air and were bounced all over the sky by some rough weather. This set the seal on the rest of the flight, which we survived on a diet of awful coffee and regular prayers."

Undaunted by her past experiences, Enid decided to visit her son in San Francisco a few years later, and it wasn't long before a flight to lake Tahoe was suggested to allow for a spot of gambling. Which, considering Enid's previous run of luck, wasn't a very good idea at all!

The flight, uneventful on the outward journey, ran into difficulties over the Sierra Nevada on the return leg...

The bleak and inhospitable terrain passing below the aircraft's wings drew Enid's gaze as she stared out of her cabin window.

"All I could see was snow, rocks and pine trees," she recalled. "It didn't look at all inviting."

The aircraft began to wallow sluggishly in the freezing air and it quickly became apparent that all was not as it should be.

"The pilot suddenly made an announcement, telling us that a large amount of ice had built up on the wings and that an emergency landing would have to be made. He told us to remove our glasses and shoes, and also to be ready to jump if neccesary, when we were on the ground."

The barren wastes of the Sierra Nevada rose slowly up to meet them as the pilot fought a losing battle to stay airborne – fate, it seemed, had not yet finished with Enid Ware.

The passengers, strapped securely in their seats, began to talk nervously amongst themselves, in an endeavour to keep their spirits up.

None more so than Enid's daughter-in-law, who unthinkingly told everyone within earshot that she wasn't surprised at the plight they found themselves in, as they were flying with her mother-in-law, a real 'Jonah,' who had already seen a ship sink under her and who now seemed about to repeat the performance with the doomed aeroplane!

"The way everyone was glaring at me, you'd have thought they honestly believed it was all my fault," said an indignant Enid.

The aircraft continued to lose height as the pilot desperately tried to shake the ice loose from the wings, and Enid wondered which would prove the more hostile – the snow-covered wilderness of the Sierra Nevada, or her fellow passengers!

"The atmosphere in the cabin was very tense, but suddenly the aircraft seemed to lighten and lift upwards very quickly." recalled Enid.

The pilot lost no time in telling his relieved passengers that he'd managed to clear the ice and set course for San Francisco, where they all eventually landed without further mishap.

'Jonah' she may have been called but, nonetheless, the gambling halls of Lake Tahoe could have done with Enid Ware's luck!

For everyone who has spent a considerable amount of time flying as a passenger, a kaleidoscopic set of images will spring to mind whenever they are asked to recount their experiences. Specific little incidents will crystallise, be they of a frightening emergency, a bumpy landing or even a particularly tasty meal. My own memories are overshadowed by the adventures recorded in this book, yet they will forever remain as a fond reminder of happy times spent aloft. Memories evoked by such incidents as my first flight...

The aeroplane chosen for this momentous milestone was an *Auster* four-seater monoplane engaged on ten shilling trips around the bay at Butlins Holiday camp, Clacton. The year was 1959.

I'd spent a great deal of my time staring enviously at the little aeroplane as it flew constantly back and forth on its fifteen minute pleasure trips, not daring to hope that I might experience the joy of my first flight before the end of our holiday.

I couldn't bring myself to ask for that long-awaited dream to be fulfilled—at thirteen, I was beginning to realise, at last, that money wasn't always easily obtainable. Dad had saved long and hard for this, our first real family holiday, and ten shillings seemed a great deal to ask of him.

I held out until the day we walked into the camp reception area and passed in front of the pleasure flight booking desk. The large advertising poster, showing a richly illustrated scene of the Auster in flight, drew me like a magnet.

"Can I go flying, dad?" I asked quickly, sticking close to my mother for support.

"If you want, son," he said and turned towards the booking desk.

It's difficult to describe the emotions I felt as I watched dad striding towards the pretty young redcoat selling the tickets.

Excitement, astonishment—even a little thrill of fear now that the moment had arrived to take to the air.

"I think I'll go as well," said mum, which made me feel a lot better.

"Two tickets please, for my wife and boy," said dad to the girl at the desk.

Dad did not share my enthusiasm for flying!

"What's the matter with you then? Are you yellow?" replied the redcoat, with scant regard for his finer feelings.

"Three tickets," grated dad, drawing himself up to his full six feet.

We were led out to the middle of a large, none too even field where the *Auster* stood waiting, its engine ticking over. Dad was bundled into the front seat alongside the pilot whilst mum sat with me in the rear of the aeroplane. The doors were slammed shut and the *Auster* began to move quickly over the bumpy surface.

We were being bounced about considerably by the time we'd reached flying speed, which made the take-off even more remarkable.

We suddenly seemed to soar into the air – the bouncing ceased abrubtly and my dream became a reality.

The pilot banked the *Auster* out over the sea and I could see dad looking fixedly ahead as though to blot out the sight of the ground so far below.

I was in a state of complete euphoria; it was the greatest moment of my life and I was sharing it with my mum and dad. The pilot was a God to me – I'd watched him every evening as he'd flung the *Auster* about the sky in every aerobatic manoeuvre it was capable of. It was his way of letting off steam at the end of the day.

All too soon, we were turning back towards the airfield and the *Auster* began to descend. Then we were dropping quickly down, the field seemingly growing larger by the second.

We landed with a thump and bounced down the field for what seemed a long time before rolling to a halt.

We clambered out, thanked the pilot and started to walk away. I paused for one last look at the *Auster* and overheard the pilot talking to his ground mechanic.

"You'd better check those brakes before we take the next lot – I thought we were never going to stop just then!"

Mum enjoyed the flight, but admitted to me in later years that she had been a little apprehensive as the aircraft banked over the sea.

"I couldn't swim at the time," she told me with typical Yorkshire logic.

Mum has flown on several occasions since.

Dad stopped buying aeroplane tickets from pretty young redcoats and never flew again!

Another memory is of being hoisted aboard a *DC-3*, three sheets to the wind, along with the rest of the Penang Parachute Club and strapped into a metal bench seat specially fitted for our use. We had provided a well-received demonstration jump at the Malayan town of Ipoh and had enjoyed the hospitality of its people to the point of falling down. The *DC-3* was to fly us back to Penang.

As it took off into the teeth of a torrential downpour, the tail yawing from side to side, the rear door, directly opposite our position, sprang open. I can remember clearly the shriek of the wind as it howled through the cabin and the look of relief on the face of the crewman who eventually managed to get it closed again.

The *DC-3* was, and always will be, my favourite aircraft.

Memories of my first flight on a *Comet 4* conjure up visions of a proud young stewardess sitting opposite me, balancing a threepenny piece coin on its edge to demonstrate the smooth flying capabilities of 'her' aeroplane. The coin stayed upright for fifteen minutes.

Here are The opening words of a steward as he welcomed an all male trooping party on board a New Zealand *Bristol Freighter.* This was the first time I'd ever flown in this aircraft and I'd been regaled with rich stories of its noisy, rivet popping performance.

"Gentlemen, good morning. In the likely event of a crash landing...!"

Sometimes, passengers have more than their fair share of troubles before take-off. Others even have problems getting out to the aeroplane in the first place.

A Stroll Around The Pier

Prior to modernisation in the late 1970s, the piers at Gatwick Airport were little more than corridors with removable side gates to allow access to either the steps leading down to the tarmac, or the movable tubes—used to link pier to aircraft. On the day in question, British Caledonian passengers were waiting at the gate to be ferried out to their aircraft by coach.

Unlike the normal type of coach, this vehicle had a detachable passenger section similar to an articulated lorry, with the driver having no control over the doors. These were operated by push-button from within the passenger compartment. Ensuring that everyone was safely seated, the driver set-out for the aircraft which was waiting some distance away on the apron.

Halfway across the tarmac, he stopped to allow a taxing aircraft to pass, continuing on his way when it was safe to do so.

On arrival at the foot of the aircraft steps, the ground crew discovered that the coach was empty. A frantic search revealed the missing passengers wandering far and wide over the tarmac, where they'd been stranded by the unsuspecting coach driver.

When he'd stopped for the taxiing aircraft, his passengers had wrongly assumed that they had arrived ready for boarding and had let themselves off the coach.

It took three-quarters of an hour to round them all up again!

Standard procedure going slightly astray led to the next incident.

The coach driver had been alerted by check-in staff that all the passengers had booked-in ready for their night flight, and would shortly be making their way to the pier gate ready for collection.

He then proceeded to pick up the ground stewardess whose job was to meet the passengers, check their boarding passes and accompany them on to the coach. They duly arrived at the pier but found, to their consternation, that it was deserted. After waiting a short while, they radioed the check-in desk to query the delay and were told that the passengers had been sent out early by mistake and should have been at the gate already.

Both the driver and stewardess conducted an immediate search of the area and eventually found their missing charges—crammed into the pitch black confines of a movable tube!

The problem had arisen as the stream of passengers arrived at the pier gate. Expecting to find a welcoming stewardess, they had been thrown into confusion by her absence and sought to locate the aircraft themselves. Unfortunately, they had mistaken an aircraft at the gate (parked up for the night and in total darkness) as theirs, removed the chain guarding the movable tube and crowded in.

When the stewardess located them and attempted to explain the mistake, the irate passengers refused to believe her and wouldn't move, insisting that they were in the right.

After a long argument, the stewardess finally won the day by pointing out that the aeroplane they were all so intent on boarding didn't even belong to British Caledonian!

Eventually, the disgruntled passengers were boarded on the correct aircraft and took-off somewhat later than anticipated.

On another memorable occasion, a Caledonian employee, walking along the south pier, met a lady wheeling a pushchair. She asked him where her flight left from and he politely replied that she wanted the centre pier, pointing it out to her in the distance.

A few minutes later, he spotted her calmly walking across the tarmac towards the centre pier, dodging around taxiing aircraft in the process. The baby, it was rumoured, slept right through his perilous outing.

Meanwhile, back at the check-in desk...

"I'm afraid that's a little large for hand baggage," explained a patient receptionist to the Nigerian couple facing her over the counter.

"I don't understand," wailed the distraught wife. "We were told we could take one or two items with us as cabin baggage."

"Well, I'm very sorry, madam but our interpretation of cabin baggage is a little more conservative than yours, and I'm sure you'll appreciate that if everyone took a fridge-freezer on board we'd be in real trouble!"

Once on board, there is a chance to relax and strike up a conversation with your neighbour or, in some cases, make new friends. A convivial drink over dinner helps to ease the tensions of pre-flight preparations and the chance of a relaxing sleep in the reclining seat is an added bonus.

An idyllic and civilised way to enjoy a flight by anyone's standards – but beware. Even indulging in this simple luxury can cause an international incident!

In Flight Fracas

A Trans-World *Jumbo Jet*, five miles high over the Atlantic, droned peacefully towards Heathrow, its complement of passengers enjoying the quiet pleasures of a trouble-free flight. For one of them, the time had arrived for a gentle snooze and, with a sleepy nod to his wife, he pressed the seat recliner button. The seat tilted back, bringing forth a cry or indignation from the man behind.

"This chap leaned forward to complain about his legroom being taken up," revealed a fellow passenger, "I don't know quite what happened next, but it looked like he accidently fondled the breasts of the other man's wife as he tried to tap him on the shoulder."

Misreading the aggrieved passenger's intentions, the enraged husband jumped to his feet and sought instant justice.

" The next thing we knew they were both on their feet engaged in fisticuffs," continued the witness. "It was incredible – they were a couple of middle-aged guys, but they were going at it 'hammer and tongs.'"

The two ageing combatants caused so much mayhem that the captain radioed ahead to Heathrow and asked for the police to be standing-by when he landed.

After a desperate struggle, the two men were eventually seperated, but not before they had inflicted severe cuts and bruises on each other.

On arrival at Heathrow, the two apologetic adversaries were relieved to discover that no charges were to be brought against them – a decision that was greeted with some relief by the airport police.

"The incident happened on a foreign aircraft flying over international waters," explained a spokesman. "Technically speaking, we had no jurisdiction."

Unsavoury though this incident may have been to all concerned, there is at least one man alive today who has good reason to be thankful that he was 'mugged' by a man with a knife whilst flying.

Pensioner, Jack Sykes, was on his way to Texas, accompanied by his wife, Averina, when a piece of chicken-bone from his inflight meal became lodged in his throat.

"He started choking and couldn't dislodge the bone," said a neighbouring passenger. "An urgent request for a doctor was put-out, and the next thing I knew, this guy had rushed forward."

Charles Plotkin was a United States Air Force anaesthetist by trade and realised straight away that unless immediate action was taken, the 88 year old Briton would die within minutes.

"He asked if anyone had a knife on them and, luckily, someone produced a Swiss Army knife, the type with all the different blades," continued the passenger. "He opened it up and went to work, cutting a hole in Jack's neck."

The thirty-two year old major, working speedily and with deft skill, located the offending bone and pushed it clear with his

fingers. He then concentrated on getting Jack's breathing going again and finally bandaged the throat wound he'd inflicted.

The jet made an emergency landing and Jack was whisked off to hospital in Memphis, where he made a full recovery within four days.

"I never even got the chance to thank him," said Jack regretfully. "Without him, I'd have been a 'gonner'"

And it's not often you go looking for a man to thank him for cutting your throat!

Passengers are not all of the fare-paying, mercy of the chancellery variety, and you could be forgiven if you drool in envy at that other breed who seem to be forever jetting off on low cost exotic holidays because of their association with the airlines.

I'm referring to that much maligned and oft-misused passenger minority—the staff member.

"Worked 'ard all me life to save up for a trip in an aeroplane and those buggers are back and fore every week for nuffink," sniffed one economy class traveller.

"No wonder air fares are so dear. What with every off-duty pilot, stewardess and assorted minions flying for gratis, what can you expect?" huffed another.

Staff travel is an undoubted bonus for all who qualify, but is it really the gateway to heaven imagined by outsiders? Is it just a matter of clicking your fingers and hopping on to the earliest flight available to your particular choice of destination, or is it just another myth, perpetrated by jealous purse-string zealots?

Consider the case of one, Sylvia Knowles, receptionist for British Airways and decide for yourselves.

Somewhere In America

Accompanied by husband, Michael and children, David (7) and Geraldine (9), Sylvia flew out to Los Angeles for a well-earned holiday. She had chosen Los Angeles because there were two regular evening flights out, and her chance of getting on were that much better. Concessionary flights are given subject to availability, and do not merit top priority by any stretch of the imagination.

"When it was time to return, we turned up at Los Angeles, only to be told that there were no flights available," recalled Sylvia. "No problem. It's not unusual, so we booked into a hotel for the night and duly presented ourselves at the airport the next day."

The Knowles were again informed that there were no vacancies and returned once again to the hotel.

"On the third day, we still couldn't get on," continued Sylvia, "but this time I told them that I had to get back for work, and suggested that they split our party up if that would help. It did, and I flew back the next day, leaving Michael and the children to follow on."

Two days later, Sylvia was still waiting for her missing family.

The problem had compounded itself as soon as she left for home. The moment she, as the staff member, had left her party, their standby priority for a flight had dropped dramatically.

"Michael tried for two more days at Los Angeles, without success," said Sylvia. "After that, he decided to fly to San Francisco to see if he could get a return flight from there. He couldn't, so on they all went to Seattle."

By now, Michael, David and Geraldine had seen more of America than the Apollo astronauts and, owing to airport security regulations, Sylvia had no way of knowing their whereabouts.

"They eventually flew on to New York where they managed to get on a London bound flight," she smiled. "We had a lovely reunion, four days after I'd left them."

Airlines have long recognized the importance of the fare-paying passenger. Be they first or economy class. Every effort is made to ensure that comfort and safety are theirs for the price of a ticket, and that journeys afar are now within the reach of most pockets. Passengers are profit, livelihood and necessity, but they are also far more; As all successful airlines quickly discover...

Passengers are people too!

Chapter 6

Strange Customs

There's nothing wrong with Her Majesty's Customs and Excise – they're just normal members of the Gestapo going about their duties!"

This cutting remark is attributed to James Bond author, Ian Fleming and no doubt followed a painful meeting with the revenue men from which he emerged a sadder, wiser man. Others, not so well known, have been heard to wholeheartedly endorse the author's sentiments in varying degrees of coarseness, and countless thousands of them have every good reason to curse the professional skills displayed by modern-day customs officers.

It's a combination of these skills, dedication and endless patience that produce results of staggering proportions in the field of contraband smuggling. In one year alone, (1988-89) over six thousand seizures, amounting to a street value of £200 million were made in Great Britain.

A total of 42,637 kilograms of cannabis and 351 kilograms of cocaine was seized with 2,519 arrests made. Of these, sentences were passed on 1,349 offenders, ranging from one to twenty-five years. They are now serving terms of imprisonment amounting to 3,772 years.

37,174 litres of alcoholic drinks, 250,616 cigars and well over ten million cigarettes were confiscated with several well-organised criminal groups being broken-up in the process.

These startling figures, representing the results of just twelve months work, clearly highlight the awesome task faced by the men and women of Her Majesty's Customs. No longer are they the romantic figures of yesteryear, locked in conflict with boatloads of piratical smugglers on storm-swept, moonless beaches, and it would be foolish indeed to underestimate their professional competence.

The arrival of the aeroplane as a means of carrying passengers between different countries brought fresh problems to customs officers, and it's worth reading the report submitted by Mr. A.S. Williams, Collector of Customs and Excise at Dover on 25th July, 1909 – the day that Louis Bleriot entered the history books as the first man to fly across the English Channel...

'I have to report that M. Bleriot, with his monoplane, successfully crossed the Channel from Calais this morning, and landed in a meadow at the east side of Dover Castle about two miles from our watch house, shortly after 5am, having occupied 33 minutes in crossing.

A wireless message was conveyed to our officers announcing his departure, but he was flying at such a height that they could not trace him with a telescope.

I visited the site where he landed at 6.30am and got into conversation with a individual largely interested in the Wright aeroplane, who gave it as his opinion that although airships will never come into commercial use, there are great possibilities in store for them, and I think that a time may come when the department will have to treat their arrival seriously, and take steps to ensure that no opportunity be given for revenue interests to suffer through indiscriminate landings of airships in this country.'

Mr. Williams, having no precedent for the receiving of aircraft for customs purposes, treated the machine as a yacht and received a stern reprimand from his employers for taking the matter seriously.

His foresight proved considerably more accurate than that of his superiors, however, and he certainly outshone the individual who considered that airships would never come into commercial use.

Apprehensive passengers have been disembarking from aircraft into the arms of customs officers ever since.

The concealment of contraband and the determined efforts of would-be smugglers to avoid detection have produced some memorable moments over the years, normally ending in triumph for HM Customs. It would be wrong to suggest that they are never caught-out and they would, themselves, be the first to admit that they are far from infallible. On the other hand, they are a highly-trained team, well-versed in the dubious methods employed by contraband con-men, whose expertise and flair are enough to strike a thrill of fear through the hearts of even the most hardened smuggler.

"Most of us develop a sixth-sense or 'smugglers eye' as we call it," revealed a spokesman. "We can usually spot an amateur straight away by their mannerisms, and even some of the professional couriers can come unstuck."

What then, are the tell-tale signs to look for?

"There are any number of give-aways," I was informed. "People are either too casual, too cheerful, or too noisy. Dark glasses are a favourite trick to hide the haunted look in the eyes, but are as much of a clue in themselves."

The dark glasses brigade may well have read about the 'blink factor' but they needn't have bothered. The average person usually blinks at around twenty to thirty times a minute under normal circumstances. Nervousness can dramatically increase this number though and, even worse for the offender, attempts to forcibly control this trait result in an even bigger increase in the blink rate.The blink factor has trapped many a watery-eyed smuggler.

"Perspiration on the back of the hands, biting lips, wringing of hands, (melodramatic but it actually happens) and even the way people walk, can provide clues for our officers," continued the spokesman. "One man was hobbling so much that it drew attention to his footwear. When examined, it was discovered that he'd carried out his own, very amateur, bit of cobbling and had concealed several diamonds inside the false heels he'd nailed on."

Amazingly, false heels are still a favourite hiding place for the amateur. Especially women. "Without wishing to appear sexist, we usually find that women make better smugglers," he confided. "In fact, according to a survey of customs officials in seven European countries, women make much better smugglers than men. Their nerves are stronger, they're more cunning, and are quite untroubled by conscience. When stopped, they tend to be fluent liars and, as a last resort, will turn to either tears, hysterics or appeals for male gallantry."

Age is no barrier either. In 1987, a 73 year-old great granny was jailed for smuggling £7,000 of cannabis in her wheelchair. It was her second offence. At the other end of the scale, a young mother was arrested after drugs were found concealed under a bandage on her baby's arm.

'For gawd's sake, Lil, tell them they really are your own.'

Womens bra's have contained nearly every type of contraband except bullion, whilst unscrupulous dealers have been known to stuff diamonds into live eels in an attempt to avoid detection.

One hundred and forty dead goldfish, part of a consignment of 12,000, were found to be stuffed with heroin contained in condoms. The seizure, at San Francisco Airport, netted a catch worth over a million pounds on the black market!

Animals themselves are often subject to the smugglers greed, and rare species of birds, lizards, tortoises and other exotic animals regularly come into the country illegally. Sadly, many die on the journey. Others are more fortunate...

The Tortoise and the Weather Girl

A couple recently returned from Turkey with a tortoise, claiming to have rescued it from a gang of local children who were using it for target practice. They told customs officers that it was their intention to give it to an aunt as a pet, and duly applied for an import licence. The licence was refused when it was discovered that the tortoise they'd rescued was on the endangered species list and not even allowed as a private import unless the importer could prove it had been a family pet for many years. This little animal (a spur thigh tortoise) was believed to be no more than two years old, and desperately in need of a good home and a suitably qualified keeper.

Salvation came from an unusual source – weather girl, Wincey Willis. Known to millions of television viewers for her cheerful forecasts and sunny personality, she is perhaps not quite so well-known for her other speciality: Wincey is a herpetologist, or, in layman's terms, an expert on tortoises.

The weather girl was delighted to help, and is now the proud owner of a very lucky, if somewhat shell-shocked and bemused, spur thigh tortoise.

Then there came the case of 'Brian' the sniffer tortoise...

Brian had been seized at Heathrow under the endangered species act and, according to rumour, had been placed in a room containing several packets of cannabis to which he had reacted violently. The press, eager as ever for a good story, were told that experiments with the tortoise had shown conclusive proof that it possessed an excellent sense of smell.

Brian's handler stated that the tortoise had several advantages over dogs, and "Wouldn't be surprised if they replaced them completely in the fullness of time."

"They are a lot cheaper to feed for a start," he informed assembled reporters. "We can get away with one lettuce-leaf a day as opposed to several tins of dog food."

He went on to extol the virtues of his prodigy with some considerable enthusiasm and pointed out that Brian could "Easily be carried around in a handbag or shoulder bag."

"Admittedly, some tortoises may not be of much use in a chase," conceded the amiable handler, "but a medium-sized one could easily be hurled fifty yards to bring down a fleeing suspect."

Suspicion finally set in, and one reporter warily asked when Brian could be expected to begin his duties.

"April the 1st, Sir," replied the deadpan handler.

Hissing Sid and the Spirit Lady

A West Indian lady, passing through the green, nothing to declare channel at Heathrow was stopped by a suspicious customs officer and asked to open the large hold-all she was carrying.

As he rummaged around the top layer of assorted clothes, they suddenly began to writhe around in his hands. With unbecoming haste, he retired to a safer distance and demanded to know what the lady was carrying in the hold-all.

"My spirit," came the mysterious reply.

At that point the slithering form of a 12ft python emerged from within the hold-all and coiled menacingly alongside its owner, who claimed it was part of her exotic dance routine.

With more than a little trepidation, the pale-faced customs man continued searching the hold-all, having first ensured the python was safely out of reach.

His bravery deserved a result, and it came in the form of two kilos of herbal cannabis hidden at the bottom of the hold-all.

The lady was escorted to the interview room where she told officers that the snake was her 'spirit', and that she only did what it told her. She then refused to say any more unless the snake was present!

Unofficial sources claim that the ensuing interview with a, by now, extremely annoyed python in attendance, did nothing at all to promote the fearless, 'laughing in the face of danger', image of Her Majesty's Customs and Excise!

Animals have long been the innocent victims of human greed or ignorance but, thanks to a little known operation run by British Airways, and the tireless efforts of BA engineer, Rod Hall, they now stand a better chance of survival than ever before.

BA's 'Assisting Nature Conservation' scheme, formed in 1983 at the suggestion of Rod Hall, began airlifting illegally imported wildlife back to their native countries for release into the wild.

Thanks to the co-operation between HM Customs and British Airways, thousands of rare birds, mammals and reptiles have now been returned to their natural habitats where they rightfully belong.

Rod Hall's magnificent efforts in support of this scheme, carried out entirely in his spare time, have won international recognition from conservation groups everywhere.

Amateur smugglers still present the biggest challenge to customs officers, with usually very little to show for their pains other than the odd extra bottle or pack of cigarettes. Some of the antics played out in front of the desks however, would bring credit to any amateur dramatic group in the country.

"I've seen them crying, begging, praying, threatening and calling on every God imaginable to protest their innocence," claimed one customs man.

"We still get some punters trying to go through the green channel with huge great bottles of Scotch, under the pretext that they thought they were allowed one bottle of spirits," he continued. "Some of the more determined ones will put a dog collar on or even dress as a priest in the hope that such holy men will be above suspicion."

Unfortunately for one man, dressed as a Catholic priest, his disguise proved his undoing.

"We found almost three hundred watches concealed in a lady's girdle around his waist," I was informed. "He received a fine for the watches but was slung into prison for smuggling whilst disguised in Holy Orders."

Others will try the evasive, gift of the gab, approach, as

customs man, Clan McAllister recalls...

"The Monday morning Dublin flight into Heathrow usually managed to bring one or two assorted characters along with it," he remembered. "One of them staggered past me with two huge suitcases and I called him over for a check. He wasn't too pleased but parked his suitcases in front of me for inspection."

The conversation developed along familiar lines.

"Could you tell me what you've got in your cases, sir?" queried the customs man.

"I could that, sur," replied the Irishman, "That one's empty and this one's got nothing in it." his genial smile took the sting out of the situation but Officer McAllister persevered.

"Yes, very funny, now what have you got in there."

"Ah, Jasus, they're only toys for the kids," came the reply.

"Right, that's fair enough, now perhaps you'll be so kind as to tell me what they are," asked Clan, beginning to see light at the end of the tunnel.

"Certainly, sur. A boy and a girl," came the light-extinguishing reply.

Customs officers are only human and it should come as no surprise that they have their own little failings from time-to-time. Thankfully, they don't usually cause too many problems but, just occasionally...

I had just returned from a long tour of duty in the Far East and stood before an unsmiling customs man at Heathrow. He ferreted through my luggage with a great deal of enthusiasm and emerged triumphant with my prized Olympus camera.

I'd bought the camera at the start of my tour and the ruling at that time, if memory serves correct, stated that any item of this nature purchased over two years prior to re-entering the country would be duty-free.

"When did you buy this?" he barked.

"Over two years ago," I replied with as much hurt in my tone as I could muster.

"It looks brand new to me," he shot back. "How do you explain that?"

"Because it's spent most of that time in the pawn shop," I answered. "I've got a dated receipt for the camera if you'd like to see it."

"Dated receipts are the easiest thing in the world to get hold of," came the rejoinder.

"Well, I'm sorry but what else can I offer to convince you?" I pleaded.

"Nothing at all," came the sarcastic reply, "Go on, I'll let you off this time but I don't believe one word you've told me."

As I staggered thankfully away a smiling customs officer stopped me.

"Don't worry about him, son," he explained, "He's the chairman of Chelsea Football Supporters Club and his team took an awful hammering yesterday. He's always like that when they lose!"

At least my accuser didn't suffer the same fate as one of his counterparts at Cairo Airport. This unfortunate man was transferred from his post for having an "unnaturally depressing face."

Justifying his action, a senior officer said customs men were supposed to greet passengers with a smile, not to give them the impression that customs procedure is a frightful ordeal.

Other failings can be found in the four-legged members of HM Customs...

A North Sea oil rig worker, passing through customs with just a hold-all in his possession, suddenly became aware that a large golden labrador was taking a great deal of interest in his progress.

The labrador, one of an elite team of drug detector 'superdogs' had then surprised his handler by breaking loose and pouncing on the alarmed man's hold-all. The burly oilman tried to pull it free but, with great tenacity, the growling dog hung on until his handler appeared on the scene.

Advising the oilman that he suspected him of harbouring an illegal substance, the customs officer took charge of the hold-all and opened it up. As he did so, his superdog dived forward and snatched a small white parcel from amongst the bag's contents.

Instead of allowing his handler to take it from him however, the dog dashed into a corner and began tearing at the parcel with great gusto. When the customs man finally managed to prise it loose from the reluctant jaws of his faithful companion, the 'illegal substance' was discovered.

"Chicken sandwiches!" groaned the customs man in acute embarrasment.

Apologies were quickly made to the grinning oilman whose lunch had proved so irresistable to the shamefaced handler's labrador. Far from being annoyed he promptly suggested that the hungry dog be allowed to finish his lunch.

'Superdog' needed no second bidding.

Innocent passengers are sometimes, inevitably, caught up in the web of intrigue surrounding contraband smuggling and will forever harbour feelings of deep resentment against HM Customs for subjecting them to the indignity of a strip-search (or worse). Guilty passengers, alternatively, will slip through the net and congratulate themselves on their good-fortune. Either way, customs lose, but the margin of this loss is constantly narrowing.

It may never close completely.

If it doesn't, it will not be through lack of trying.

'Shall I wipe the smile off his face, or will you?'

Look out for these exciting, new titles from Brooks Books

air to weave a rich tapestry of courage, skill and high endeavour. At the other end of the scale, celebrities of stage and screen offer their own, often amusing, look at their qualifications for receiving the award.

A percentage from the sales of every copy will be donated to the Royal Association for Disability And Rehabilitation.

Publication date: October 1991
Casebound, 272 pages plus photographic sections
£14.99. (prov.) ISBN: 1872706 08 8

HOW TO ORDER

You may order direct from us. We accept cheques/postal orders payable to Brooks Books, or you may pay by Access/Visa or Mastercard. In the UK, postage is £1.00 per book. Overseas, please add £4.00 per book ordered for Air Mail delivery.

A full list of our titles is available for an SAE.

We welcome trade enquiries.

Write to: Customer Services Department, Brooks Books, 23 Sylvan Avenue, Bitterne, Southampton, Hampshire, England. SO2 5JW.

We look forward to hearing from you, and hope you have enjoyed your book.